Quality & Customer Satisfaction

Tools for Measuring the Customer's Total Experience

By Maria Gisella Conca and
Antonella Pamploni Scarpa

First Edition

Quality & Customer Satisfaction

Janet MacCausland, Graphic Design and Layout

Cathy Kingery, Editor

GOAL/QPC
12B Manor Parkway, Salem, NH 03079-2862
800.643.4316 or 603.890.8800
Fax: 603.870.9122
E-mail: service@goalqpc.com
www.goalqpc.com

Printed in the United States of America

First Edition 10 9 8 7 6 5 4 3 2 1

ISBN 1-57681-059-3

Foreword

It is obviously important for organizations to attempt to improve customer satisfaction and loyalty. But it is equally important for an organization to use adequate methodologies and tools to better understand and meet its customers' needs and expectations. Corporate policies regarding customer satisfaction must be based on solid and rational grounds, and an organization's approach to fulfilling these policies must be lean and simplified.

This book is intended to help small and medium-size organizations increase their quality and customer satisfaction, two items that the "Vision 2000" protocol bring closer together.

This innovative book combines the ideas of the two authors, Maria Gisella Conca and Antonclla Pamploni Scarpa, with the case histories of several business managers.

I would like to thank Luciano Franzini and Renato Carioni, owners of Salvi S.p.A. and Rentex S.p.A., respectively, who consulted with the authors and me regarding this book. I also owe special thanks to the authors, to Cecilia Capellaro and Fabrizio Lain (from Assolombarda) for coordinating the project, and to the Milan Chamber of Commerce for their significant financial support.

Marzio Dal Cin
President of Consorzio Qualità

About the Authors

Maria Gisella Conca

Maria teaches quality management at the LIUC Cattaneo Castellanza University and is a high-level-management trainer for LRA and SDA Bocconi, two leading research institutes. She has been teaching corporate strategies and quality management for sixteen years. A prolific writer, Maria has presented numerous papers on total quality management at several important national (AIDEA, AICQ) and international conferences and meetings (EOQ, ISESAO). She has a degree in business administration and is a member of the International Teachers Programme HEC in Paris and a visiting professor at the Tokyo Hitotsubashi University.

Antonella Pamploni Scarpa

Antonella is Director of Human Resources and Customer Satisfaction Manager for Fujitsu Services S.p.A. and president of the Italian Association for Quality Centronord. She has served as an instructor for several major national (RAI, ENEL, AICQ, CESI) and international (Group ICL, Symbol, Lanier) institutions. Antonella is a frequent speaker at conventions and roundtable discussions on human resources, customer satisfaction, and quality and business effectiveness. She has a degree in the humanities and has taken the Strategic Human Resources Management & Leading Organizational Change Course from the University of California–Berkeley.

Combining their extensive academic experience with practical management practices, Maria and Antonella have collaborated to provide training and consulting services for many years.

A Word from the Authors

This workbook illustrates a methodology for measuring customer satisfaction and includes results from activities done in conjunction with a number of member firms of the Quality Consortium in Milan. It combines diverse techniques—such as using customer-focused strategies, knowledge of quality systems, and excellence self-assessment methodologies—with the field expertise of three visionary business managers who provided their case histories (see chapter 10). The experiments and field research, which were conducted over a one-year period, allowed us to accommodate the methodology outlined in chapter 5 to the specific needs of small and medium-size organizations.

We hope that business owners, managers, consultants, and all those who consider customer satisfaction the key element for success—in profit-oriented and not-for-profit organizations alike—will find this book an incentive to improve their business activities.

We owe special thanks to the Milan Chamber of Commerce, for its financial support, and to Cecilia Cappellaro and Fabrizio Lain of the Assolombarda and the Quality Consortium, for the mutually beneficial relationship we have developed over the years with them.

Thanks also go to the business owners who enthusiastically believed in the project throughout its duration; to ICL Italia S.p.A., for the documents they provided; to Sergio Meacci from Databank and Marco Bignoli from Eurisko, for their valuable suggestions; to Alessandro Boin, Andrea Cortese, Christian Indelicato, Michele Lanza, and Elisa Scarpa; and to Simona Tripoli, our ally in the search for the best communication style, for her creativity.

Preface by Giovanni Mattana, President of National AICQ

In recent years, a great deal of focus has been placed on customer orientation. But the practices necessary for meeting this paradigm have not been easy for small and medium-size organizations to adapt.

The reasons for this are many: These companies have limited resources; it is difficult for a company to implement "soft" customer-oriented business practices when it is used to implementing only product-oriented practices; and customers are not always available to help.

But ISO 9000:2000 requires a customer-oriented approach. Therefore, all companies wishing to maintain their ISO certification must comply with these requirements, which oblige them to ascertain their customers' needs and expectations and satisfy them.

There is a tremendous need among small and medium-size companies for a set of simple and effective tools to successfully adapt a customer-oriented approach. To this end, this book provides an analysis of the ISO 9000:2000 requirements, describes some useful tools, suggests a model for their implementation, and describes an experiment the authors conducted by applying the methodology described herein to three small companies.

Understanding the customer and his/her needs and successfully satisfying them is the underlying theme of this book. With the help of a strategic classification diagram, the attributes of customer satisfaction are identified and put into questionnaire form. Practical tools are presented that can help small and medium-size organizations listen to the customer, analyze customer-related data, and make the best use of this information to continually and systematically improve their relationships with their customers and achieve better business results.

Two other key aspects of the book are an explanation of pitfalls to avoid and the aforementioned three case studies of small companies that have applied the methods outlined herein.

My best wishes go to all organizations pursuing strategies toward becoming customer-driven, and to the authors for continued success.

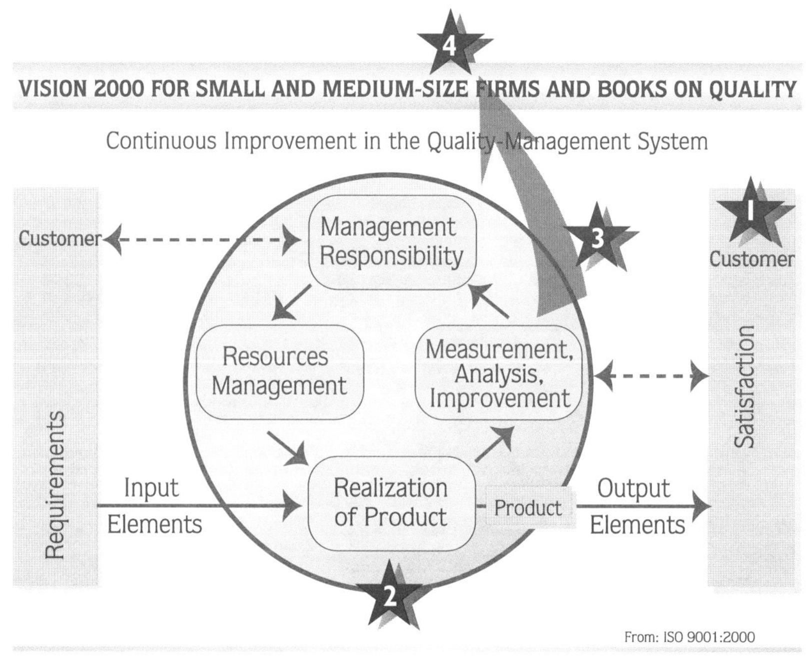

 Quality and Customer Satisfaction

 Management by Processes

 Improvement, Innovation, and Benchmarking

Vision 2000 Certification

Contents

Chapter One

Customer Orientation

- Before you begin
- Customer satisfaction for small and medium-size firms

Before You Begin

The self-assessment test in chapter 4 and some of the exercises in this book are intended to assist the business manager in finding the many improvement opportunities that can result from actively listening to the external customer. The ideas presented herein are based on our personal experience gained from our training and consulting activities, as well as state-of-the-art knowledge that can be applied to small and medium-size organizations.

We believe that learning is an ongoing process; therefore, we suggest using this book as a foundation, keeping in mind that many aspects herein have been simplified to provide organizations with an easy path to follow as they discover the many opportunities for improvement that lie ahead.

In this text, we adopt a "facilitator" approach and avoid attempting to provide definitive solutions. The legend at right explains the icons that are used throughout this book.

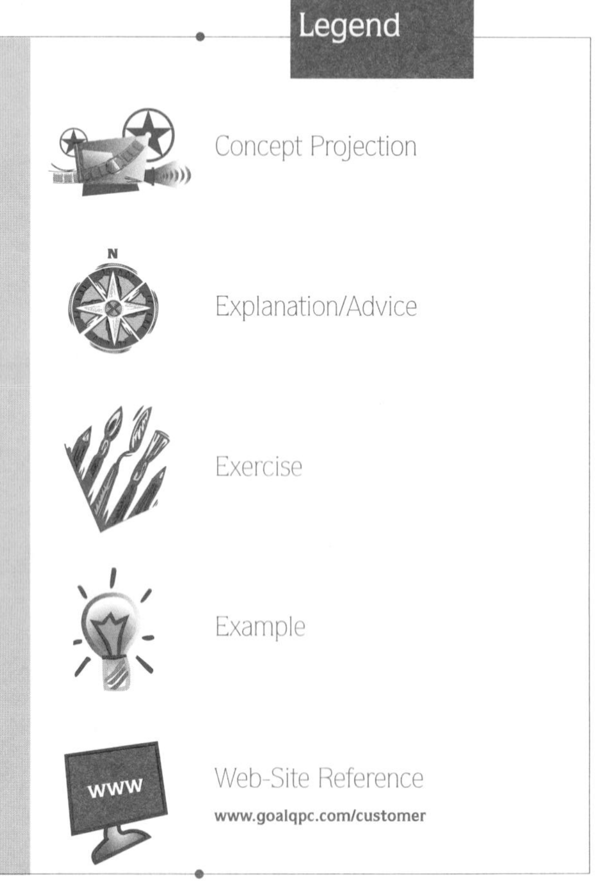

Customer Satisfaction for Small and Medium-Size Firms

To understand the scope of this book, an examination of the characteristics of today's small and medium-size firms is necessary. Small and medium-size businesses make up a substantial part of today's economy and provide a significant contribution to employment and to industry.

The definition of the term "small and medium-size business" usually takes into account several factors, including number of staff members, amount of annual profit, and value-added by manufacturing activities or fixed asset values. The European Community, for instance, defines small and medium-size businesses as those having a maximum of 250 employees and an annual profit of up to 50 million euros; small businesses, on the other hand, employ less than 50 people and have an annual profit of up to 10 million euros.

Small and medium-size firms operate differently from one another. Therefore, it is necessary to consider many different factors (e.g., whether a firm's manager is also the owner of the business, and the level of flexibility achieved through a "learn-by-doing" approach) when performing business assessments.

These aspects aside, today's small and medium-size firms often discover customer needs by using a reactive approach, whereby they respond to customer demands rather than having customers participate in the design of new products and services. With a true customer-oriented approach, the organizational behavior is more proactive. This means that the process whereby the organization understands its customers' needs and expectations begins with the voice of the customer.

Numerous methods exist to collect customers' opinions: focus groups, in-person and phone surveys, mailings, brainstorming, customer panels, and databases. There are also many different sources for obtaining this information: fairs, exhibitions, internal and external organizational events, visits by sales representatives, technical assistance, complaints, visits to other firms, news from industrial or consumers' associations, meetings, and so forth.

Small and medium-size businesses often use only a few of these tools to understand whether their customers are satisfied. The most commonly used tool is the questionnaire, which is often adapted from another firm's questionnaire and is sent by mail or electronically. Often these businesses do not use any methods to obtain customer evaluations of their performance.

To improve its customers' loyalty and increase its competitiveness, an organization should properly structure the customer data it collects so it can define its action priorities based on the importance customers assign to certain attributes (explained in chapter 6).

Finally, customer satisfaction must be managed and planned for the medium and long term. It must be linked to performance indicators of an organization's primary business processes. It must address the organization's development and competitiveness goals.

The Purpose of This Customer Satisfaction Book Is to..

Stimulate the transition of small and medium-size firms from:

Customer-
SEEKING
Organizations

Customer-
ORIENTED
Organizations

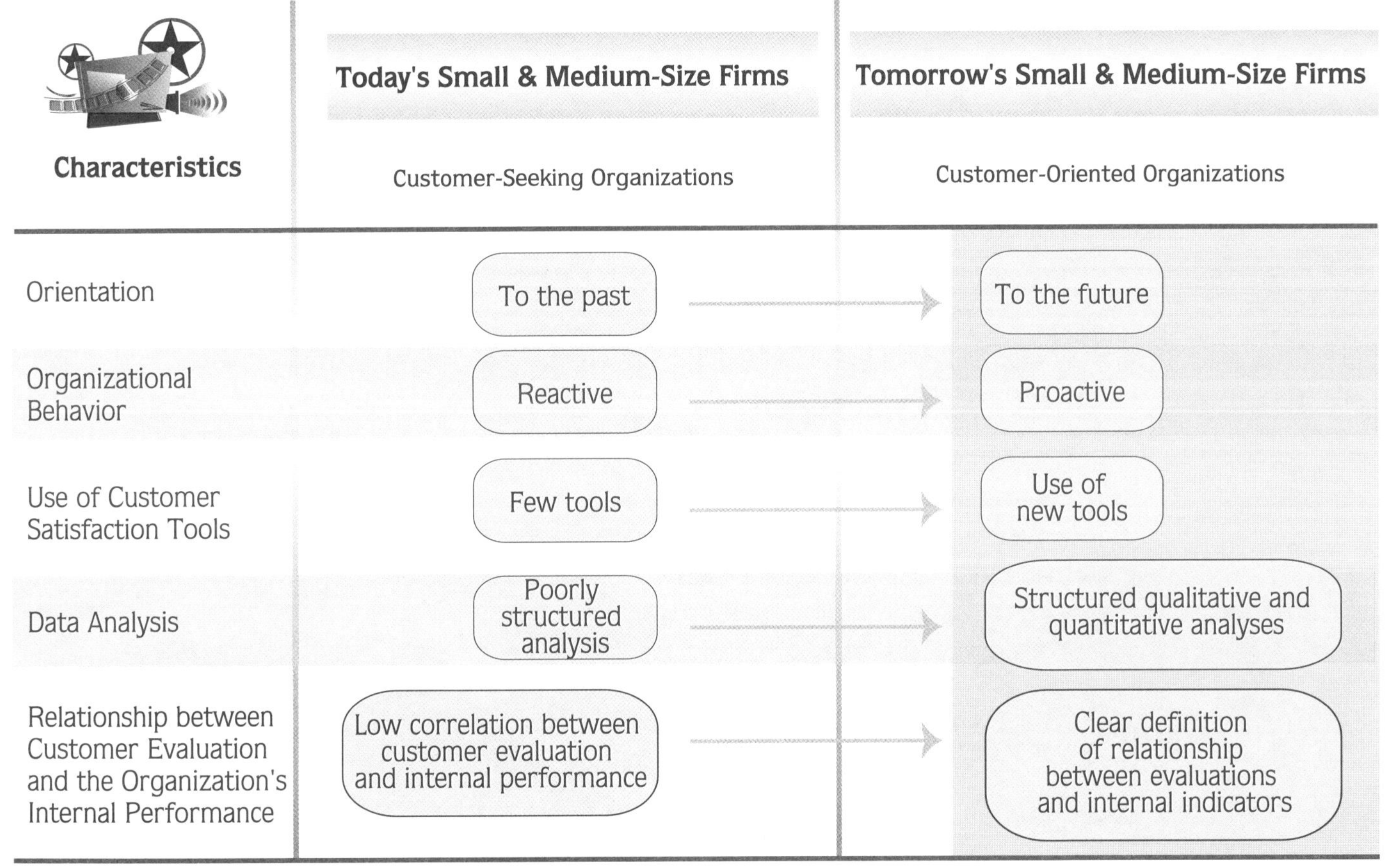

Characteristics	Today's Small & Medium-Size Firms Customer-Seeking Organizations		Tomorrow's Small & Medium-Size Firms Customer-Oriented Organizations
Orientation	To the past	→	To the future
Organizational Behavior	Reactive	→	Proactive
Use of Customer Satisfaction Tools	Few tools	→	Use of new tools
Data Analysis	Poorly structured analysis	→	Structured qualitative and quantitative analyses
Relationship between Customer Evaluation and the Organization's Internal Performance	Low correlation between customer evaluation and internal performance	→	Clear definition of relationship between evaluations and internal indicators

Customer-Oriented Organization

Core Activities

1. Understand customer's needs and expectations about product performance, delivery, prices, the product's capability to increase customer's competitiveness, etc. (See chapters 1, 2, and 3)

2. Disseminate information concerning the need within the organization to effectively meet such needs and expectations (See chapters 4 and 5)

3. Measure customer's satisfaction and plan improvements through the use of collected data (See chapters 6, 7, 8, 9, and 10)

Chapter Two

The Customer

- The hierarchy of customer needs
- Developing relationships with the customer
- How to look at quality
- Reasons to measure customer satisfaction

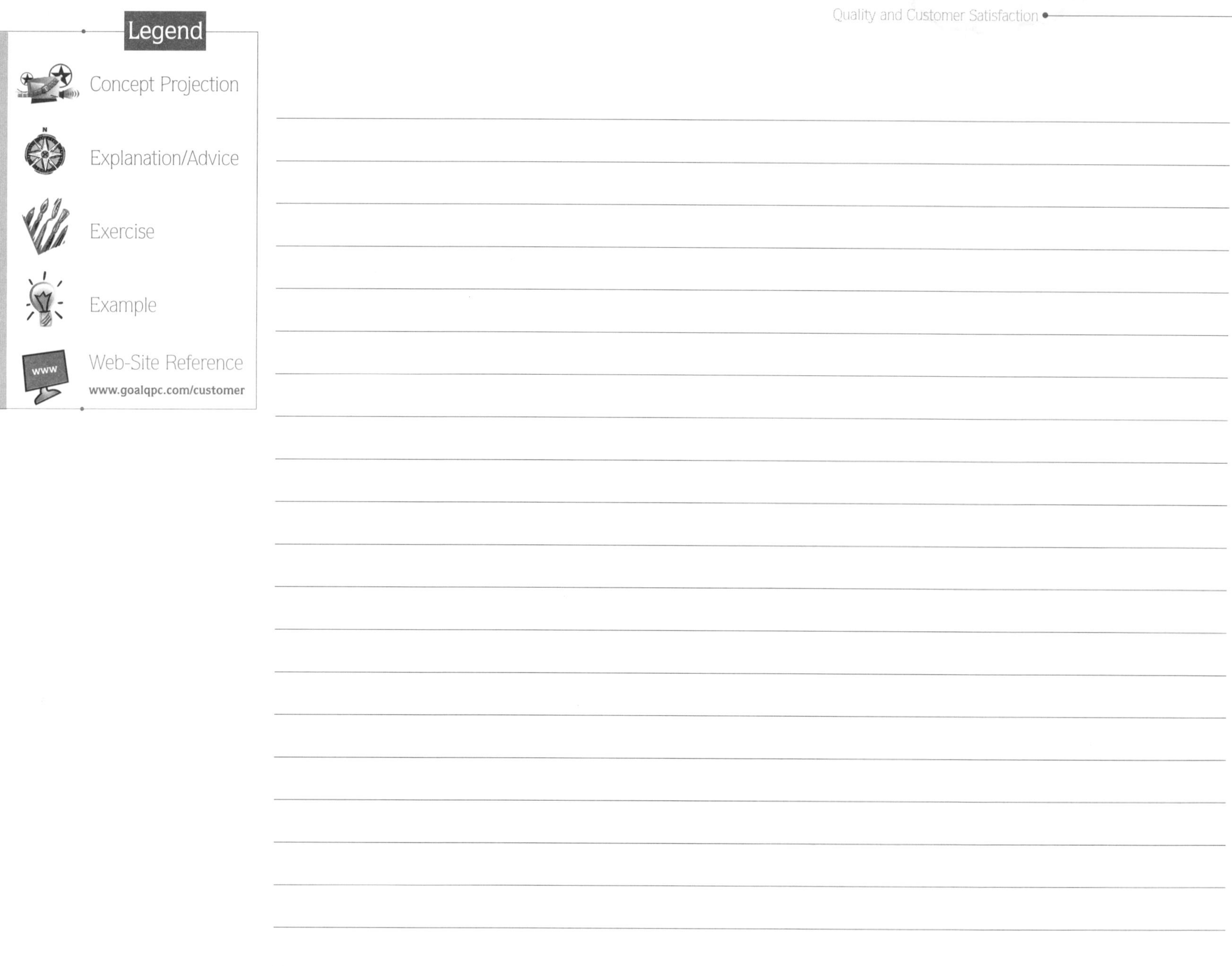
Legend
Concept Projection
Explanation/Advice
Exercise
Example
www
Web-Site Reference
www.goalqpc.com/customer

The Customer

Who is the customer? The ISO 9000:2000 standard provides the following definition: an organization or individual receiving a product. Another definition is as follows: The customer is a subject who receives products or services from an organization, based on the agreed-upon contractual requirements. But such simple definitions do not fully reflect the current competitive corporate environment or the strategic decisions that organizations must implement to meet or exceed customer expectations, whether stated or implied.

Today's customer is very different from the customer of decades past. Various definitions of today's customer include such descriptive phrases as "very demanding," "very informed," and even "a monster." We see today's customer as many-sided, colorful, imaginative, flattered, respected, beloved, and feared. We realize that the customer's realm extends all over the world, thanks to the many different communication tools available today, such as the internet.

The customer's primary power is his/her ability to choose—a power that can determine an organization's life or death. The principal goal of an organization is to satisfy—or, better yet, delight—the customer. An ideal partnership between organization and customer results in the customer's becoming a faithful and trustworthy ally on the organization's road to success.

Hierarchy of Needs*

Human Needs	Customer Needs
Self-Actualization and Personal Growth Needs	**Value Growth (Sustainable Profits)**
Transcendence and Esteem Needs	Partnership (Relationship)
Belongingness Needs	Knowledge Needs (Know-How)
Safety Needs	Service Needs
Physiological Needs	Product Needs

*Maslow—Revised by Maria Gisella Conca and Antonella Pamploni Scarpa

The Hierarchy of Customer Needs

The Hierarchy of Human Needs—a theory posited by A. H. Maslow in 1943—helps in the effort to understand today's customers. Maslow theorized that human needs can be classified in an ascending order, beginning with physiological needs and moving up to self-actualization needs.

The evolution of customers' needs follows the same course that Maslow outlined for individuals.

Product needs can be compared to human physiological needs (i.e., food, water, air, and shelter). The more a customer's specific needs are met, the less satisfied the customer becomes, since needs that are met no longer impact human motivation; they only generate needs of a higher category.

The need for a service is comparable to human safety needs (i.e., order, stability, and certainty). Having service needs met generates a knowledge need in the customer. This is comparable to Maslow's human need for belongingness (i.e., the need to be affiliated with a specific group of customers).

At this point, the transition to self-actualization (i.e., the need for self-fulfillment and success) triggers a search for partnerships, aggregations, and mergers. This brings the customer to the highest level of self-actualization—the fully fledged implementation of the relationship between customer and organization—which results in an increase in the organization's value and profitability.

A corporation's business manager plays a key role in developing customer relationships, which are discussed in the following pages.

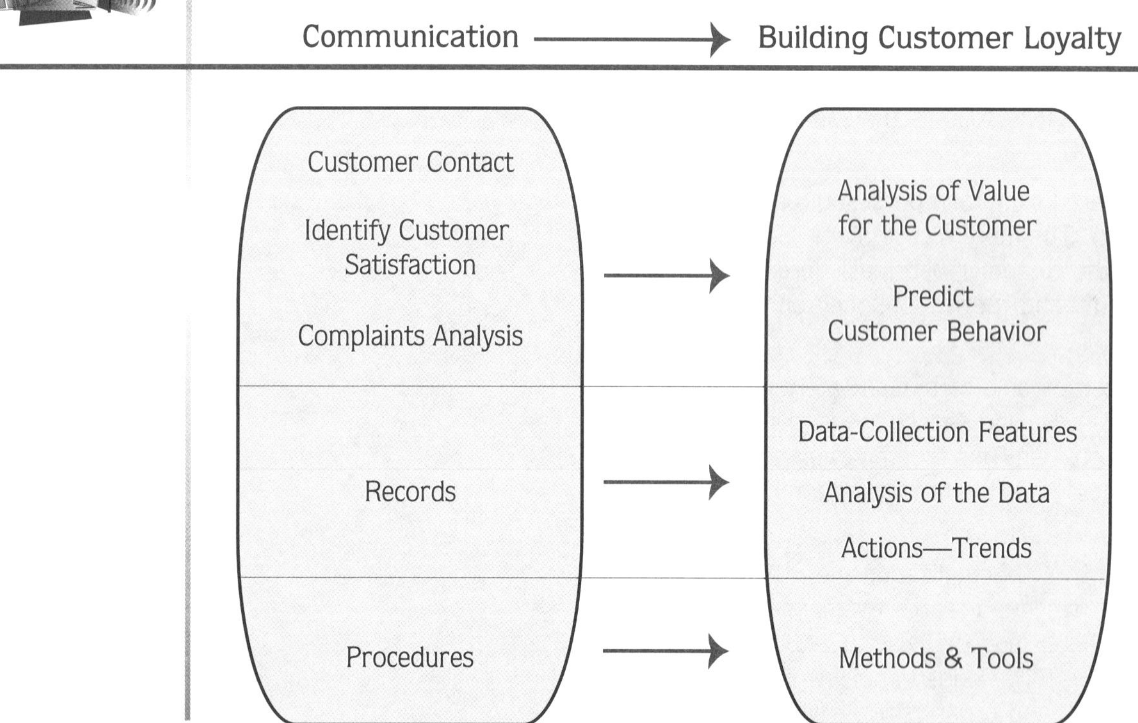
Developing Relationships with the Customer
Communication
Building Customer Loyalty
Customer Contact
Identify Customer Satisfaction
Complaints Analysis
Analysis of Value for the Customer
Predict Customer Behavior
Records
Data-Collection Features
Analysis of the Data
Actions—Trends
Procedures
Methods & Tools

Developing Relationships with the Customer

In developing customer relationships, two important goals for a business manager are communication and loyalty building. The term "communication" includes all contacts established with a customer, particularly visits in person to obtain a signature on an order or after inconveniences that might occur during a transaction. In general, all communication-based activities are useful for measuring customer satisfaction. When organizations adopt ISO standard–based quality systems, anomalies are often reported by external and/or internal customers, which leads to preventive or corrective actions. But the development of customer relationships is reactive in these cases and does not entail any dramatic changes in the relationship itself or imply analysis of future trends.

> "Loyalty building," on the other hand, entails action to analyze whatever creates value for the customer.

Customer relationships must be built on mutual trust and respect. The ability to create customer relationships based on loyalty is a must for business managers, who must also know how to communicate the value of this allegiance to the customer. The challenge consists of making it clear to customers that the organization brings value to the customer's activities and also creates value for the customer's own customers, where applicable.

An organization must develop relationships with its customers so it can better predict its customers' future behavior and, therefore, better satisfy their needs. Knowing what creates value for the customer, collecting and analyzing relevant data and information, and constantly and tenaciously adopting methodologies that are closer to its customers' approval are all essential to the development of long-lasting transactions that offer benefits to the organization and the customer alike.

> According to the American Management Association, 65% of an organization's profit comes from repeat business.

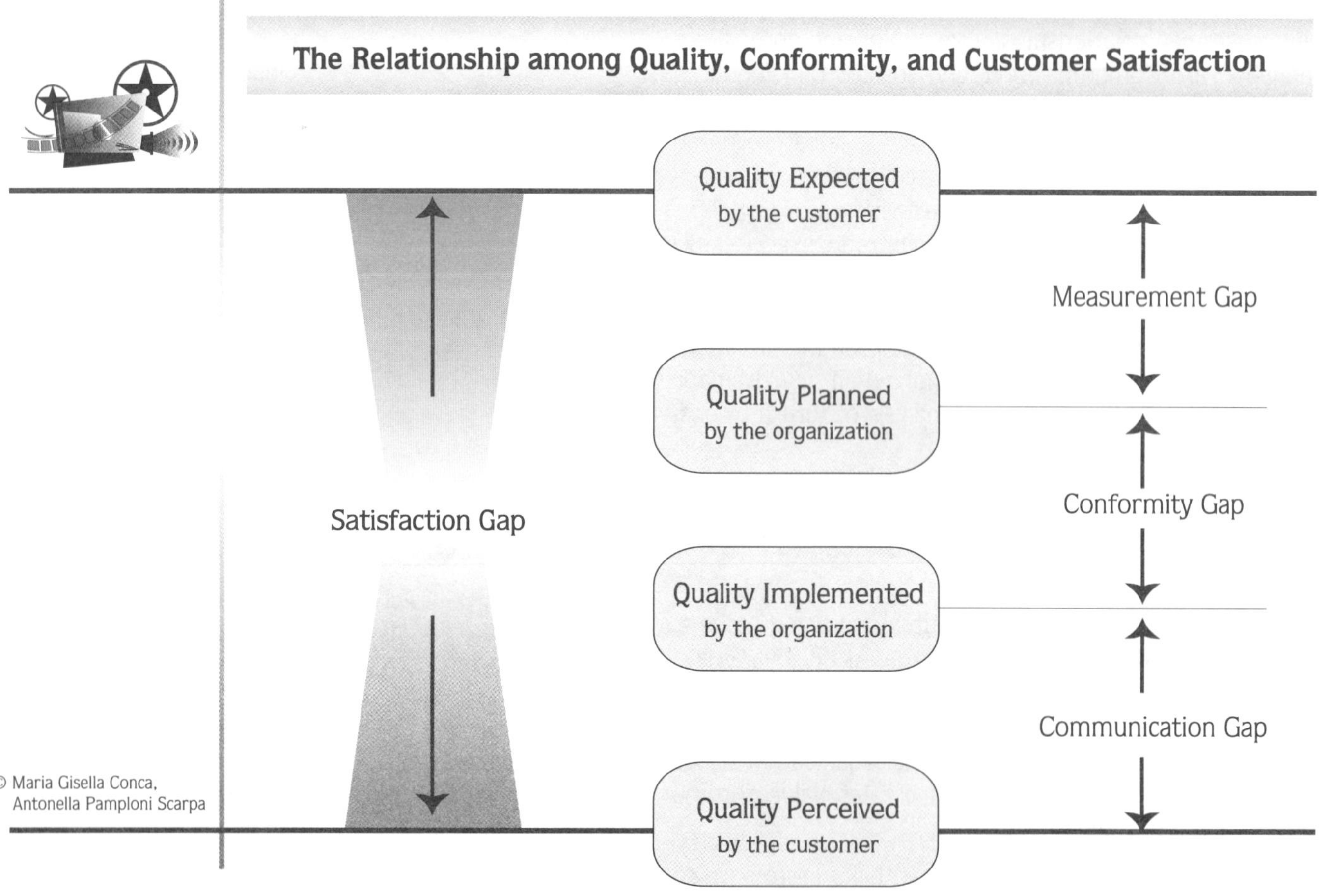
The Relationship among Quality, Conformity, and Customer Satisfaction
Quality Expected
by the customer
Measurement Gap
Quality Planned
by the organization
Satisfaction Gap
Conformity Gap
Quality Implemented
by the organization
Communication Gap
Quality Perceived
by the customer
© Maria Gisella Conca,
Antonella Pamploni Scarpa

How to Look at Quality

Quality can be assessed from many different perspectives, depending on who looks at it, how they look at it, and how they measure it (i.e., subjectively or objectively). The principal elements to be considered include the following:

EXPECTED QUALITY

- The quality that the customer expects the organization to provide in an effort to meet all customer needs, whether clearly stated or implicitly linked with the products/services purchased.

PLANNED QUALITY

- The quality that the organization plans to provide through its structures, resources, and processes after interpreting the customer's requests.

DEPLOYED QUALITY

- The result of the implementation of planned quality (i.e., the final product and/or service).

PERCEIVED QUALITY

- The level of quality that the customer believes he/she receives, as compared to expected quality.

The ideal situation is when an organization can achieve a perfect combination of these four elements and perceived quality is equal to or higher than expected quality. This results from an organization's fully understanding stated and implied customer needs; implementing appropriate structures, resources, and processes; planning coherently; and delivering the product/service in accordance with the plan. In the real world, however, the following variances are often observed with respect to these four elements:

SATISFACTION GAP

The variance between perceived and expected quality. What the customer receives does not measure up to his/her expectations.

SURVEY GAP

The customer's needs and expectations are not adequately identified, and there is a variance between planned quality and expected quality. The organization does not fully comprehend the customer's stated and/or implied needs.

CONFORMITY GAP

The variance between deployed quality and planned quality. The result of the process (i.e., the final product/service) is not exactly in line with what the organization planned.

COMMUNICATION GAP

The variance between deployed quality and perceived quality.

All these gaps result when the organization does not precisely and objectively enhance the quality of the product/service it provides. Of the four gaps listed above, the one that occurs most frequently is the satisfaction gap. This is because this gap is impacted by all the others, as can be seen from the chart on the previous page.

While planned and deployed quality are generally measured using objective tools, expected and perceived quality are often measured using subjective tools. This is an error that must be avoided. Adequate tools are available that allow for the objective measurement of customer expectation and perception, and organizations should use them.

The difference between perceived quality and expected quality determines the level of customer satisfaction. The three levels of customer satisfaction are as follows:

A DELIGHTED CUSTOMER
Perceived quality exceeds expected quality.

A SATISFIED CUSTOMER
Perceived quality is in line with expected quality.

A DISSATISFIED CUSTOMER
Perceived quality falls below expected quality.

NOTE: For further insight into customer satisfaction and a more advanced approach than the one described in this book, see the Fita-AISM document "Qualità & Customer Satisfaction: quali obiettivi per la competitività" ("Quality & Customer Satisfaction: goals for competitiveness"), by Sergio Meacci.

Reasons to Measure Customer Satisfaction

1. Investments in customer loyalty enable the organization to save money on future customer-acquisition activities.

2. By measuring customer satisfaction, the organization gives its customers the attention they deserve. This practice also helps prevent customer complaints, which cost more to solve.

3. When the organization assesses that the customer is satisfied, it can also understand why, and thus become aware of its strengths. This knowledge can then be used for communication at all levels: internal, external, promotions, and sales. It also enhances the organization's return on investment in communication and improves the organization's image.

Markets are continually evolving. To remain dynamic, organizations must constantly innovate and expand their range of products/services. The business manager must learn from the customer which direction to take before the customer decides to use other organizations' products/services.

Vision 2000 certification demands customer satisfaction measurement

If the organization is already certified, it enjoys a satisfied requirement.

If the organization is not certified, it can prepare to manage customer satisfaction and achieve considerable competitive advantages.

Legend

Concept Projection

Explanation/Advice

Exercise

Example

Web-Site Reference
www.goalqpc.com/customer

Chapter Three

Vision 2000 Certification

- A quality-management system model based on processes
- The principal rules of the ISO 9000:2000 standard

A Quality-Management System Model Based on Processes

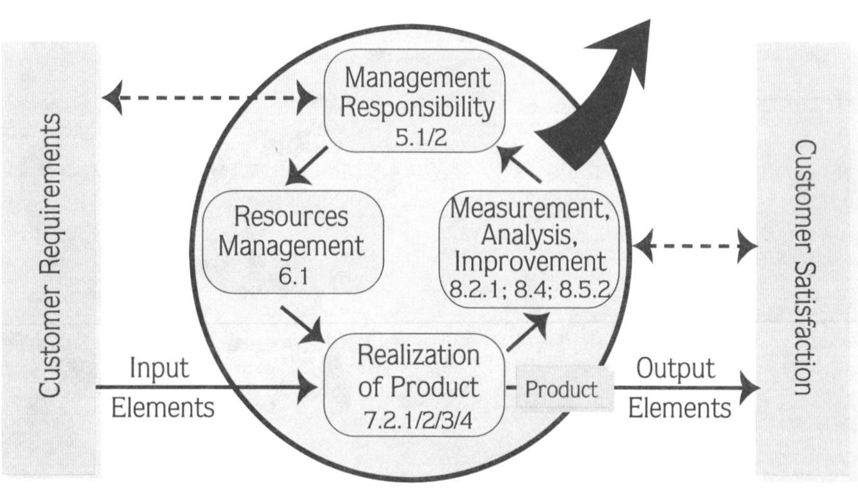

From: ISO 9001:2000, revised by the authors

A Quality-Management System Model Based on Processes

The ISO 9001:2000 standard encourages adoption of a quality-management approach based on processes.

The customer is fundamental in the ISO 9001:2000 model, which is illustrated on the previous page. The customer is the one who starts the process by putting forth the principal requirements, as well as the one who terminates the process by providing information regarding the level of satisfaction enjoyed.

The customer is explicitly referred to in the four main chapters of the standard (chapters 5, 6, 7, and 8). The ISO 9001:2000 model illustrates the major requirements that refer to customer satisfaction and attention (sections 5.2, 6.1, 7.2.1, and 8.2.1).

The Principal Rules of ISO Standards 9000:2000—Quality-Management Systems

ISO 9000:2000 includes the following international standards:

- ISO 9000:2000—This describes the fundamentals of quality-management systems and defines a vocabulary.

- ISO 9001:2000—This describes the requirements of quality-management systems. This is the standard used to demonstrate an organization's ability to provide products/services that conform to customer requirements and to the rules and policies defined by the organization. Based on this standard, an organization can request certification of its quality-management system. The certification is signed by an authorized independent body after a satisfactory inspection is conducted at the organization's headquarters and operating units.

- ISO 9004:2000—This is a guideline for the implementation of quality-management systems, including processes for continual improvement. It has a wider scope than ISO 9001, since it considers not only external customer satisfaction (as ISO 9001 does) but also the satisfaction of all other parties involved (i.e., shareholders, employees, suppliers, and the social community).

The three standards that are listed above are known collectively as "Vision 2000."

NOTE: The text on this page was revised based on Filippo Barbarino's book, titled "UNI EN ISO 9001:2000, Il Sole 24 Ore, 2001," which we suggest reading for further details and insight.

The Quality-Management Process

The following is a complete list of the eight basic principles of quality management, from which stem all other principal requirements of ISO 9001:2000:

a. Customer Orientation:

Organizations depend on their customers and should therefore understand their current and future needs, meet their requirements, and aim at exceeding their expectations.

b. Leadership [...]

c. Staff involvement [...]

d. Process approach [...]

e. System management approach [...]

f. Continual improvement [...]

g. Fact-based business decision process [...]

h. Mutually beneficial relationship with suppliers [...]

From:
ISO 9004:2000
Quality Management Systems
Guidelines for Performance Improvement (revision)

The ISO 9000:2000 fundamentals and vocabulary and ISO 9004:2000 Guidelines for Performance Improvement standards refer to quality-management principles.

The most important of these principles is:

Customer Orientation

Summary of Principal Standard Requirements

Regarding customers according to ISO 9001:2000
and customer references in guidelines (ISO 9004:2000)

Introduction: 0.1 General

The decision to implement a quality-management system should be part of the organization's strategy adopted by top management.

[...] The purpose of an organization is to meet customer requirements and expectations...

It is important for organizations and their customers to evaluate the benefits that stem from the implementation of the eight quality-management principles and to assess their impact on costs and risk management.

The statements that relate to an organization's overall performance might impact customer loyalty, operating profits (market shares), and market-response speed...

From:
ISO 9004:2000
Quality Management Systems
Guidelines for Performance Improvement
(revision)

Scope and Application

The rule states that one of the objectives of its application is to enhance customer satisfaction; this objective can be pursued through an effective system implementation and primarily by means of processes that ensure continual improvement and conformity to customer and obligatory requirements.

The main goals of ISO 9001 are customer satisfaction and continual improvement of business performance.

The objectives of ISO 9004 are the satisfaction of customers and of all other parties involved and continual improvements in an organization's effectiveness and efficiency.

From:
ISO 9001:2000
Quality Management
Systems
Guidelines for
Performance
Improvement
(revision)

Management Responsibility

5.1 Management commitment

The organization's top management shall provide evidence of its commitment to the development and implementation of the quality-management system and continually improving its effectiveness by:

a) communicating to the organization the importance of meeting customer as well as statutory and regulatory requirements;
b) [...]

In implementing a quality-management system, the business manager should take into account, among other elements, the degree of satisfaction expected by the customer.

From:
ISO 9001:2000
Quality Management
Systems (revision)

5.2 Customer focus
Top management shall ensure that customer requirements are determined and are met with the aim of enhancing customer satisfaction.
(Also see 7.2.1 and 8.2.1.)

Needs and expectations of potential customers, and all other parties involved, are among the principal elements to consider when planning a quality-management system. To determine and meet the expectations of customers and other involved parties, an organization should clearly identify its counterparts, define their needs and expectations, and communicate them, as appropriate, to the entire organization, focusing on process improvement to enhance value creation to the benefit of customers and all other involved parties.

Resource Management

6.1 Provision of resources

The organization shall determine and provide the resources needed:

a) [...]

b) to enhance customer satisfaction by meeting customer requirements.

From:
ISO 9001:2000
Quality Management
Systems (revision)

Top management should provide adequate human, financial, and infrastructural resources to continually improve the effectiveness of the organization's quality-management system and enhance customer satisfaction.

Product Realization

From: ISO 9001:2000 Quality Management Systems (revision)

7.2.1 Determination of requirements related to the product

The organization shall determine:
a) requirements specified by the customer, including the requirements for delivery and post-delivery activities;
b) requirements not stated by the customer but necessary for specified or intended use;
c) [...]

7.2.2 Review of requirements related to the product

The organization shall review the requirements related to the product, prior to its commitment to supply the product to the customer. The purpose of such a review is to ensure that all requirements are precisely determined, that any dispute between customer and supplier be resolved, and that the organization has the ability to meet the defined requirements.

It is quite obvious that the ISO 9001 regulation is intended to safeguard both the customer and the organization. The goal of this requirement is to prevent the organization from taking responsibilities that have not been adequately assessed, which could result in the organization's inability to meet its commitments, thus leading to customer dissatisfaction, and a possible loss of customers or organizational image.

7.2.3 Customer communication

The organization shall determine and implement effective arrangements for communicating with customers in relation to:
a) product information;
b) inquiries, contracts, or order handling, including amendments;
c) customer feedback, including customer complaints.

This requirement is absolutely complementary to clause 7.2.2.

7.5.4 Customer property

The organization shall exercise care with customer property while it is under the organization's control or being used by the organization. The organization shall identify and protect customer property provided for use with or incorporation into the product. If any customer property is lost, damaged, or otherwise found to be unsuitable for use, this shall be reported to the customer and records maintained. **NOTE:** Customer property can include intellectual property as well.

Measurement, Analysis, and Improvement

From: ISO 9001:2000 Quality Management Systems (revision)

8.2.1 Customer satisfaction

As one of the measurements of the performance of the quality-management system, the organization shall monitor information relating to customer perception as to whether the organization has met customer requirements. The activity shall be organized and systematic, and the methods for obtaining and using this information shall be determined.

Measurement and monitoring of customer satisfaction shall prove suitable when the organization collects customer information from all relevant sources and implements processes in order to gather and disseminate such information.
The organization may refer to any source of customer information — internal, external, written, or verbal — provided by the customers themselves (the end users, etc.); some of the main sources of information are reported as follows:

- Surveys on customers' and users' satisfaction
- Requirements specified by the customer and contractual information
- Elements linked to the provision of services
- Product feedback
- Market-demand needs
- Any useful information relating to competition

8.4 Analysis of data

The organization shall systematically determine (utilizing statistical techniques as appropriate), collect, and analyze appropriate data to demonstrate the suitability and effectiveness of the quality-management system and to evaluate where continual improvement of the effectiveness of the quality-management system can be made. This shall include data generated as a result of monitoring and measurement and from other relevant sources. The analysis of data shall provide information relating to: a) customer satisfaction (see 8.2.1), b) conformity to product requirements, and c) [...]

The organization should analyze all collected data in order to evaluate its performance with respect to defined plans, goals, and targets and decide which corrective actions to implement. Customer complaints and the results of customer satisfaction surveys are some of the information to collect in order to identify areas with improvement opportunities.

8.5.2 Corrective actions

The organization shall take action to eliminate the cause of nonconformity in order to prevent recurrence [...].
A documented procedure shall be established to define requirements:
a) Reviewing nonconformity (including customer complaints) and b) [...]

The organization should identify all relevant sources of information and collect data as appropriate in order to implement effective corrective actions. Principal sources of information include results of data analyses, customer satisfaction measurements, and results of self-evaluations.

Legend

Concept Projection

Explanation/Advice

Exercise

Example

Web-Site Reference
www.goalqpc.com/customer

Chapter Four

The Test

- A leadership self-evaluation for the business manager

The self-evaluation that follows should be carried out by the organization's business manager.

This evaluation measures leadership with respect to customer orientation.

Leadership is one of the eight principles of quality management (see chapter 3). It represents top management's ability to determine the organization's strategies (e.g., vision and mission) to create and maintain a stimulating business environment and to foster attention at all employee levels to achieving and enhancing customer satisfaction in the pursuit of the organization's business goals.

The ten simplified questions listed in the self-evaluation in this chapter were extracted from complex and extensive research conducted by the SDA Bocconi Business School and set forth in "Small and Medium Size Firms: Quality and Vision 2000," published in 2000.

The possible scores range from 0 to 10. These scores can be classified into three groups:

- 7–10: The organization's business manager has already implemented Vision 2000.
- 4–6: The business manager is aware of Vision 2000's importance, but there is little evidence of it within the organization.
- 0–3: Vision 2000 is not implemented or applied at all.

The purpose of this self-evaluation is to generate management awareness with respect to leadership. The results of the evaluation should be analyzed by the business manager, who can then implement appropriate corrective actions concerning each specific item.

After completing the self-evaluation questionnaire, you can compare your results with the ones that are shown on page 35. These are the results from a survey of thirty small businesses that are affiliated with the Quality Consortium.

Leadership Self-Evaluation Questionnaire

 Fully implemented item (7–10)	Awareness of importance but little or no evidence within the organization (4–6)	 Item not implemented/applied (0–3)

Question	Score
1. Do you conduct surveys to measure/monitor customer satisfaction?	
2. Do you prioritize your actions based on data from surveys?	
3. Do you communicate survey results to all levels within your organization? Do you involve your staff members in defining business and personal goals?	
4. Do you have a value proposition that focuses on the customer?	
5. Did you give your sales staff adequate training on how to manage contacts with the customer both in person and on the telephone?	
6. Do your senior managers know who your strategic customers are?	
7. Do you know the percentage of customers your organization acquired and/or lost in a given year and the percentage of profit they provided?	
8. Do you know the main reasons why you lost those customers?	
9. Are customer complaints of any importance to you?	
10. Is your staff informed of your organization's success with respect to your customers?	
FINAL SCORE	

TOTAL AVERAGE

Mark a score of between 0 and 10 for each question, according to the following scale:

10 = Fully applied

0 = Not at all applied

Results of the Business Manager's Self-Evaluation on Leadership	
	AVERAGE OF BETWEEN 10 AND 7: Congratulations! You are a business manager who cares about your customers.
	AVERAGE OF BETWEEN 6 AND 4: Your results can be improved. Please analyze each item of your self-evaluation and plan actions to achieve a score higher than 7.
	AVERAGE OF BETWEEN 3 AND 0: You need some education on what “customer care” is all about. Help yourself with a good book on the topic or attend some of the meetings organized by GOAL/QPC.

Leadership Self-Evaluation Questionnaire

The results of a survey of 30 businesses affiliated with the Quality Consortium

Fully implemented item (7–10)	Awareness of importance but little or no evidence within the organization (4–6)	Item not implemented/applied (0–3)

1. Do you conduct surveys to measure/monitor customer satisfaction?
2. Do you prioritize your actions based on data from surveys?
3. Do you communicate survey results to all levels within the organization? Do you involve your staff members in defining business and personal goals?
4. Do you have a value proposition that focuses on the customer?
5. Did you give your sales staff adequate training on how to manage contacts with the customer both in person and on the telephone?
6. Do your senior managers know who your strategic customers are?
7. Do you know the percentage of customers your organization acquired and/or lost in a given year and the percentage of profit they provided?
8. Do you know the main reasons why you lost those customers?
9. Are customer complaints of any importance to you?
10. Is your staff informed of your organization's success with respect to your customers?

Research conducted in October 1999 by the SDA Bocconi Business School in Milan; published in "Small and Medium Size Firms: Quality and Vision 2000."

Legend

Concept Projection

Explanation/Advice

Exercise

Example

Web-Site Reference
www.goalqpc.com/customer

Chapter Five

The Method

- The Customer Satisfaction Management Model
- Model explanation: Step A
- Model explanation: Step B

The model proposed herein has been tested with three businesses affiliated with the Quality Consortium (see chapter 10 for details).

Explanation of the Customer Satisfaction Model

The Customer Satisfaction Management Model consists of two steps:

step A, which concerns the SURVEY

step B, which deals with the IMPLEMENTATION

In step A, the model has two labels across the top: "internal communication" and "external communication." Their position in the model indicates that communication triggers activities.

Activities →

In step B, on the other hand, the "organization" label is positioned on top because an organization must be able to rapidly respond to meet and exceed customer expectations.

STEP A Customer Satisfaction SURVEY Model

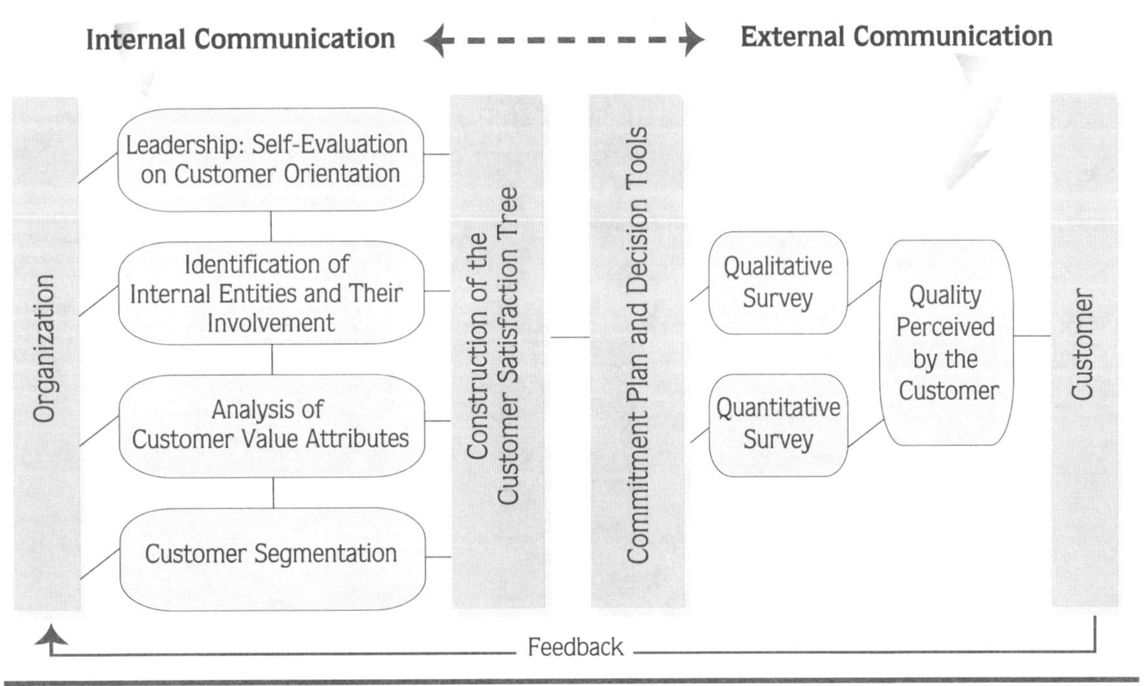

STEP B Customer Satisfaction IMPLEMENTATION Model

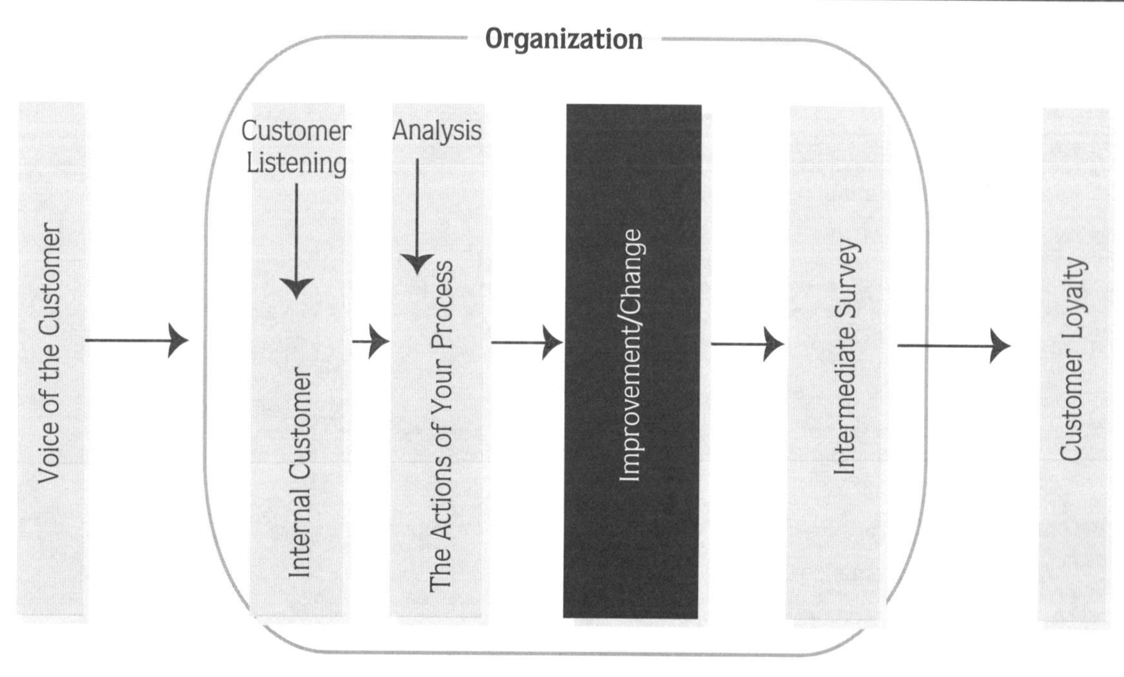

Model Explanation: Step A

Here is a closer look at the individual blocks that make up the model.

Internal communication is a means for disseminating knowledge, confrontation, and an exchange of ideas within an organization.

An organization's top management must determine corporate policies and define analyses to be carried out by staff members who must be able to interact both internally and externally with the customer to provide a qualitatively valid and timely product/service.

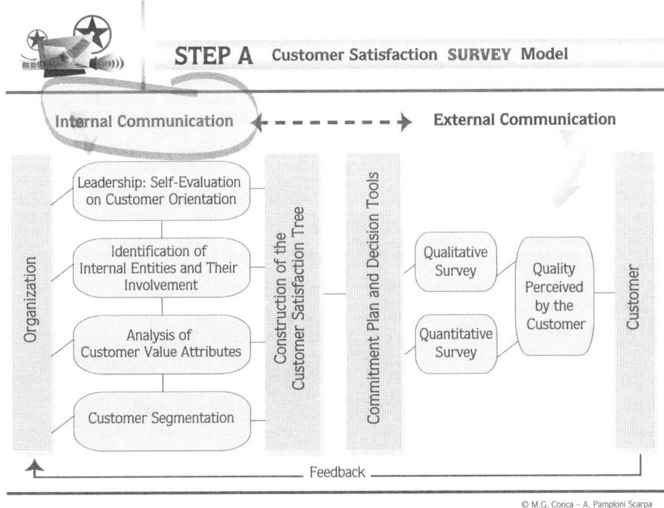

It is essential for internal communication to contribute to the creation of a working environment that allows for staff involvement in an open, flexible, and cooperative manner. One of the key elements in facilitating internal communication is the enthusiasm with which employees are invited to express their ideas and provide creative contributions.

Leadership, communication, and customer satisfaction are inseparable aspects within an organization. To be able to provide quality to the organization's customers, staff members need knowledge, recognition, support, and encouragement.

Communication, both internal and external, is a normative requirement according to the Vision 2000 clause 5.5.4, "Organization of internal communication," and clause 7.2.3, "Customer communication."

The four blocks (highlighted to the right) that appear below "internal communication" concern the following:

- **Leadership**, as exemplified by the self-evaluation exercise outlined in chapter 4.
- **Identification of internal entities** and their involvement through the creation of working groups that cooperate in conducting customer satisfaction surveys.
- **Analysis of customer value attributes**, which refers primarily to the identification of elements that the organization believes generate value for its customers (see chapter 6).
- **Customer segmentation** (see chapter 6) is intended to analyze the composition of an organization's customer population to allow for more effective survey planning (e.g., What information does the business manager want, and who should provide it?).

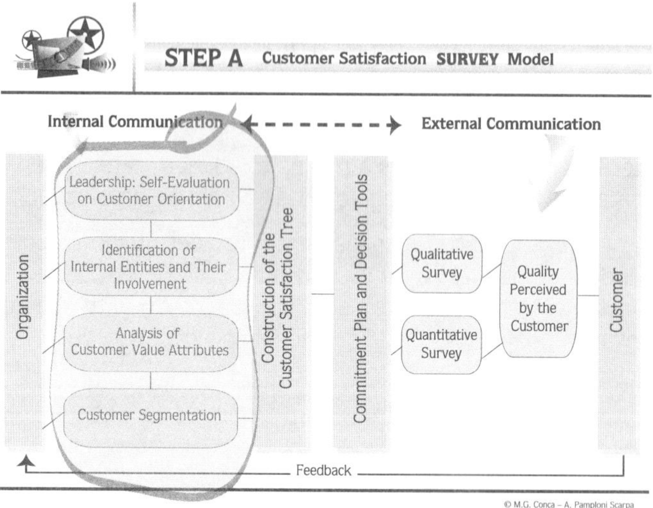

The two blocks on the left and right sides of the model refer to the two entities—the organization and the customer—that interact to achieve mutual benefits.

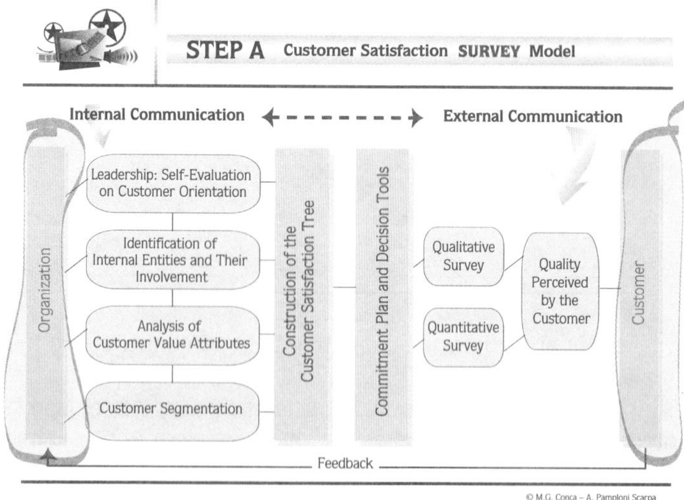

The four blocks on the left side of the figure (leadership, internal entities identification, attributes analysis, and customer segmentation) lead to the construction of a customer satisfaction tree, which incorporates all the attributes that create value for the customer.

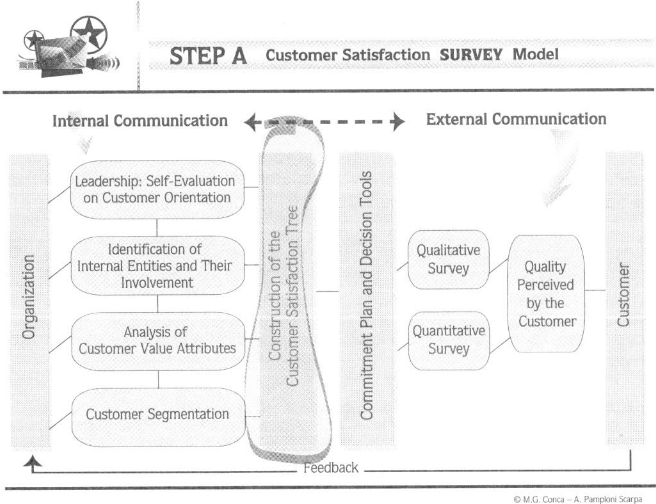

The commitment plan (see chapter 7) and the decision tools (see chapter 6) are founded on the activities carried out in these four blocks and on additional contributions made by an organization's staff members during implemention of the program. This generates awareness of the value that the customer represents to the organization.

The "external communication" portion of the figure concerns any activity the organization performs in an effort to measure customer satisfaction and related results. External communication with the customer features two important aspects: information and listening. The quality that the customer expects is based on word-of-mouth advertising, the customer's personal experience, and information received from the organization. An organization should regularly review the methods it uses to promote customer communication and reinforce its market image.

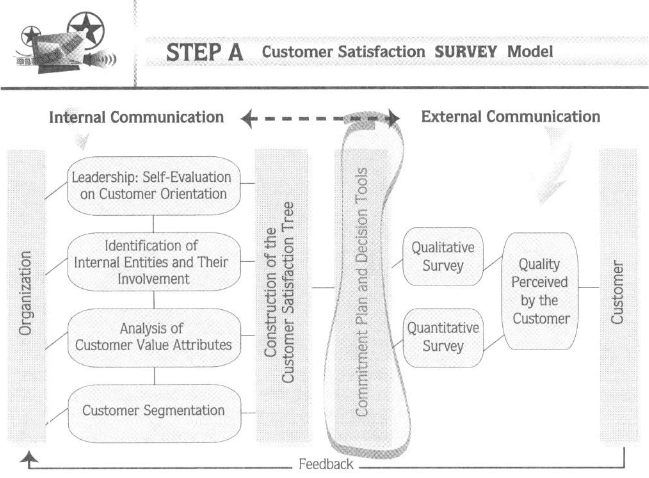

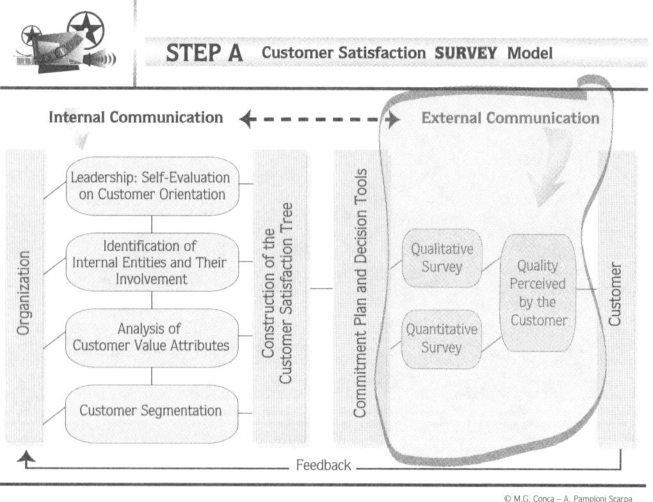

Customer listening systems include qualitative and quantitative surveys. Qualitative surveys—accomplished by means of individual interviews or collective interviews with groups of customers—allow an organization to identify the qualitative elements on which customers base their purchasing decisions. Quantitative surveys, which are the main focus of this book, are used to gather data about customers and analyze it by means of statistical tools.

The arrow between the customer and the organization (shown at right) underlines the importance of customer feedback, which allows the organization to move to step B.

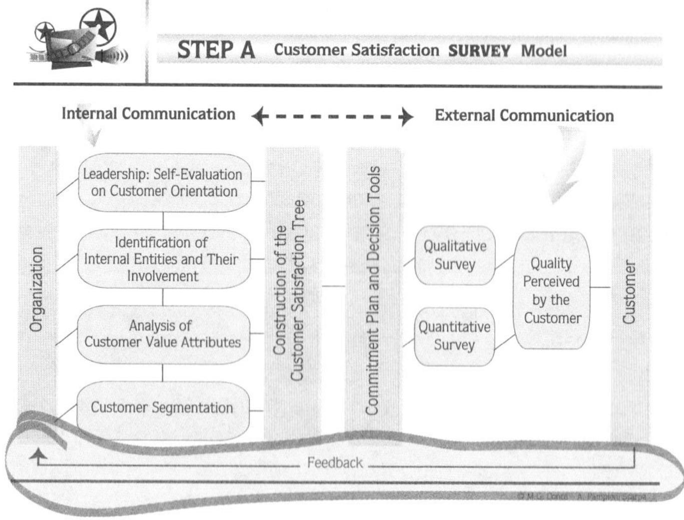

Model Explanation: Step B

In step B, the organization's task is to understand the customer feedback. The six vertical blocks in the figure progress from "voice of the customer" to "customer loyalty." Practically speaking, step B confirms that customers' needs and opinions drive the organization's strategic and structural decisions.

The first vertical block, "voice of the customer," illustrates the results of reviews, visits, or any other contacts between the customer and the organization. It shows how the customer perceives the organization and what is needed for effective communication to occur.

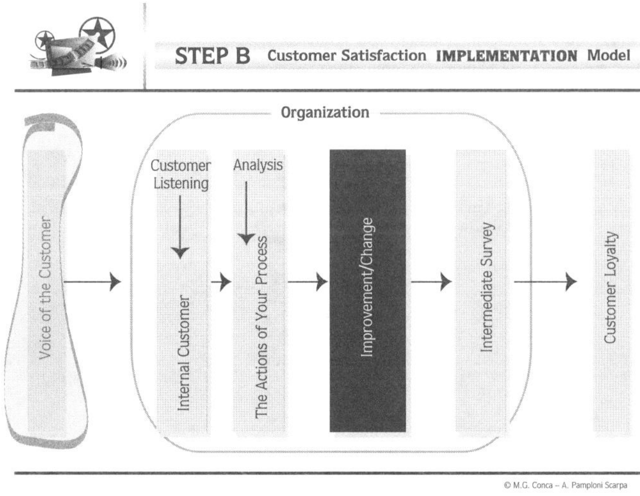

The second block, "customer listening," stresses the importance of active listening within the organization.

The focus here is on the "soft" tools, such as mission, vision, corporate values, and other similar aspects of an organization that are difficult to duplicate outside the organization.

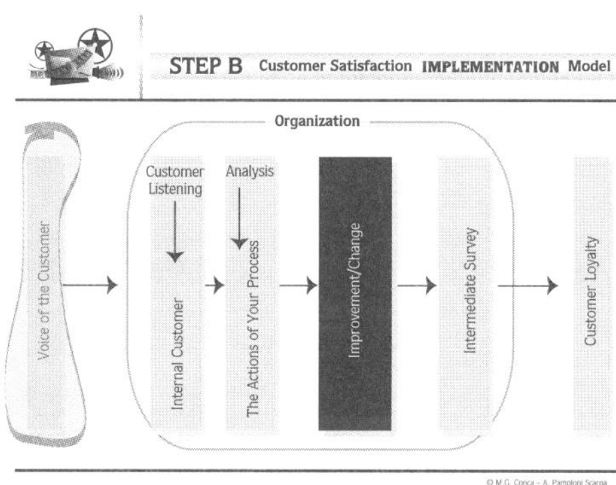

It is crucial to have a culture that fosters participation at all levels and where, after appropriate analysis is done, active listening to internal customers molds the processes shown in the blocks circled below.

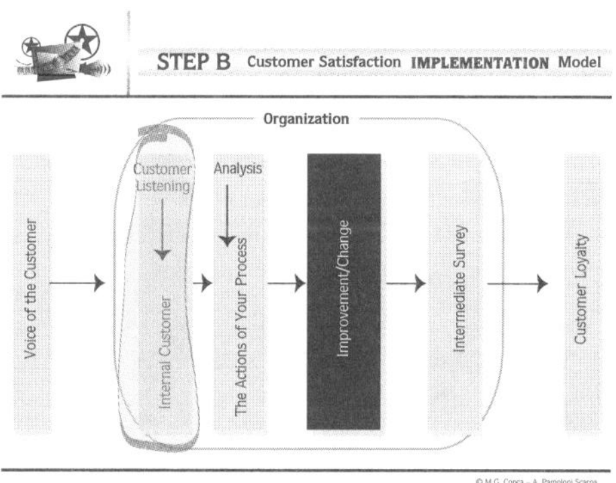

The ISO 9000:2000 standard emphasizes the role of process measurement and analysis (see chapter 3).

As an organization analyzes the way it does business and compares that to its customers' expectations, it becomes more clearly aware of its strengths and opportunities.

The heart of step B consists of two key elements:
improvement and change.

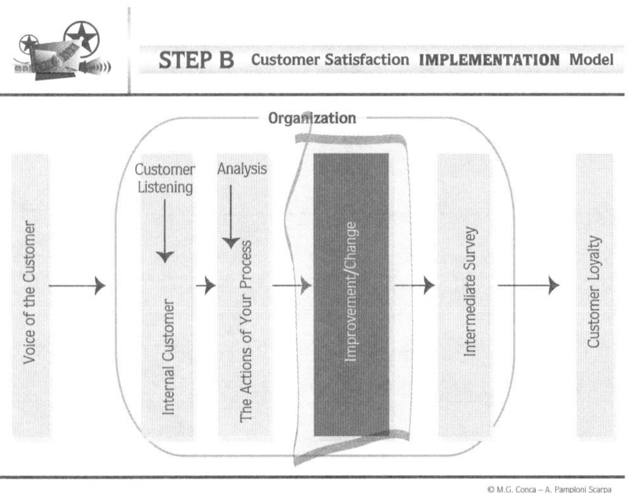

The customer decides what needs improvement and how much the organization needs to improve. Another important consideration is how quickly the organization needs to make these improvements and how quickly its main competitors can make them. An organization must be ready to continually compare itself to the best players in the industry (a technique known as benchmarking).

An in-depth analysis of an organization's business environment (and, in certain industries, its competitive status with the leading corporations in its field) is fundamental to the planning of an improvement path that will enable the organization to play a primary role in its industry.

But sometimes improvement is not enough. Dramatic changes might occur due to business transformations or global innovation processes. Amazing and delighting the customer is anything but a routine activity; it involves continual and unflagging entrepreneurial energy.

When an organization establishes a course of action based on analysis, it needs to know if this course of action will lead the organization to maintaining customer loyalty over time. Intermediate reviews, which are discussed in chapter 6, fulfill this need.

Research has shown that it is easier for an organization to improve profits by 10% through activities that affect its existing customers than it is through attempts to acquire new customers.

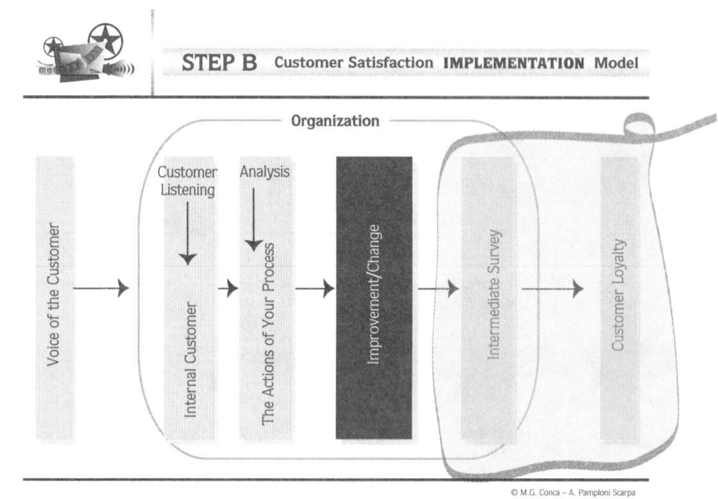

Chapter Six

The Tools

What tools should an organization use to determine customer satisfaction? Below is a list of some recommended tools for small and medium-size companies to use.

- Questionnaires
- Scorecards
- Response cards
- Complaint management
- Visits with customers
- Follow-up telephone calls
- Intermediate monitoring

Questionnaires

The authors' interviews with many business managers indicate that the preferred tool for conducting a general survey is the questionnaire. This is because the questions can be standardized and presented to all customers in the same manner.

The following pages offer suggestions for creating a questionnaire, beginning with staff involvement in identifying the questions to be asked. These are only suggestions, however, and a business manager should adjust each element for his/her specific organization as needed.

We recommend taking the following steps:

1. Identification of attributes
2. Classification of attributes
3. Construction of a customer satisfaction tree
4. Construction of the questionnaire
5. Sampling
6. Questionnaire mailing and data collection

Steps 1, 2, and 3 are fundamental elements that an organization can use when creating other survey tools.

1. Identification of Attributes

The first step in the construction of a questionnaire is to identify the attributes of the product/service the organization provides.

Hints and tips:

a. Arrange a staff meeting to identify what is important to the organization's customers. What features of the organization's product/service do customers believe to be important when deciding where to take their business? Which of an organization's activities are perceived as superior compared to those of the competition? (See the section on attribute classification for details.)

b. All meeting participants should jot down on Post-it Notes the identified attributes and indicate their job function or department. Each Post-it Note should contain only one attribute. This activity provides the business manager with an understanding of how the organization's product/service is perceived internally according to the type of job a participant performs within the organization, his/her specific sector, and the information available within the organization.

c. Read the notes aloud, grouping them based on the attributes to which they refer.

TYPES OF ATTRIBUTES

First-Level: Those that are specific to a product/service.

Second-Level: Features of a product, service, or relationship that add value for the customer.

Legend

Concept Projection

Explanation/Advice

Exercise

Example

Web-Site Reference
www.goalqpc.com/customer

2. Classification of Attributes

The fundamental attributes of an organization's product/service (i.e., first-level attributes) can change, depending on the type of organization involved. The three major types of organizations are as follows:

- **Product organizations**
- **Service organizations with product interaction** (i.e., air-transportation firms, restaurants)
- **Pure service organizations** (i.e., training, consulting services)

First-Level Attributes	Product Organization	Service Organization with Product Interaction	Pure Service Organization
	Product	Service	Service
	Service	Service/Product	Support
	Relationship	Relationship	Relationship

The two figures that follow contain second-level attributes. We suggest identifying between three and seven second-level attributes for each first-level attribute identified.

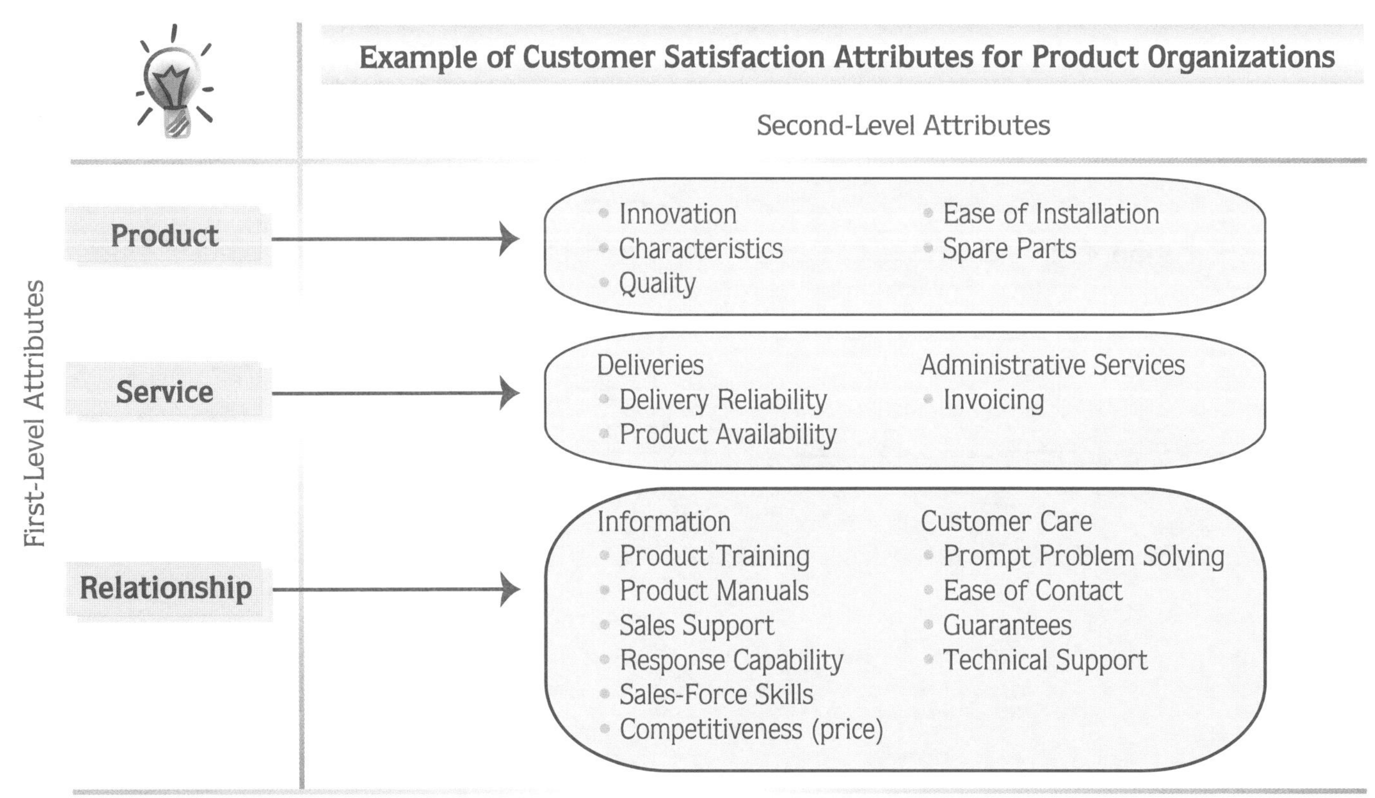

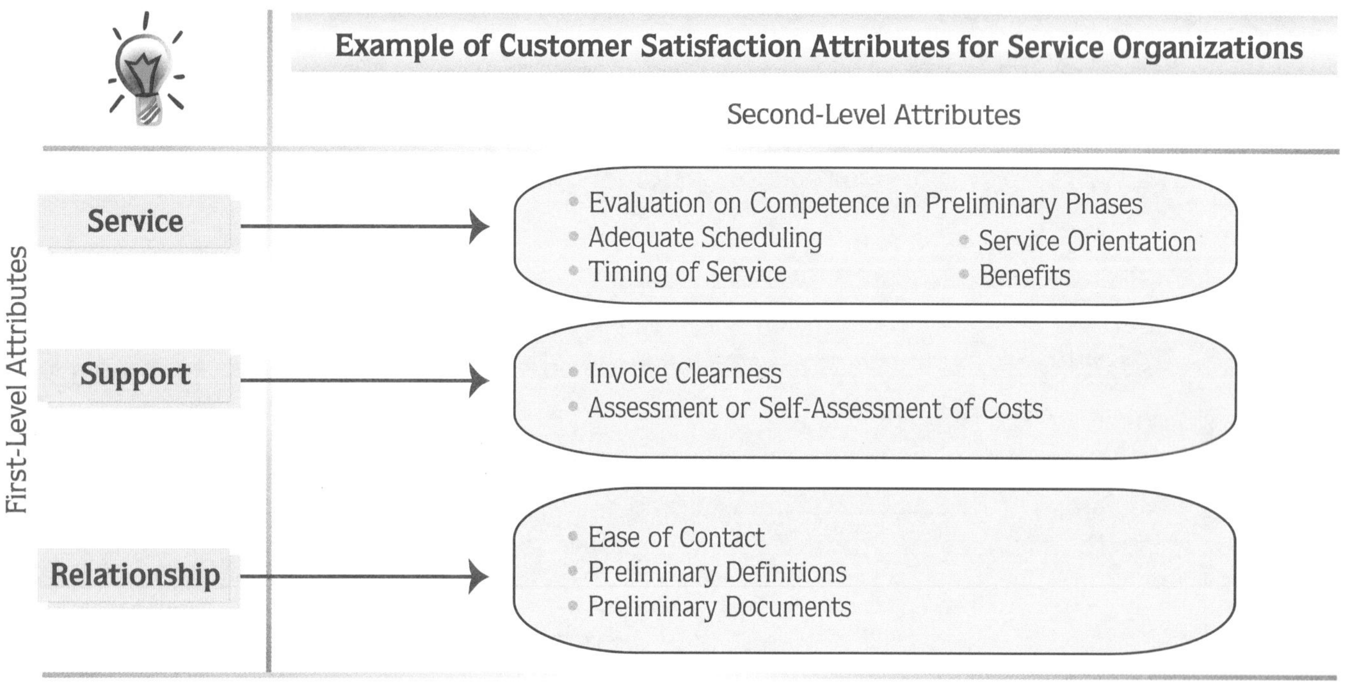
Example of Customer Satisfaction Attributes for Service Organizations
Second-Level Attributes
First-Level Attributes
Service
Evaluation on Competence in Preliminary Phases
Adequate Scheduling
Timing of Service
Service Orientation
Benefits
Support
Invoice Clearness
Assessment or Self-Assessment of Costs
Relationship
Ease of Contact
Preliminary Definitions
Preliminary Documents

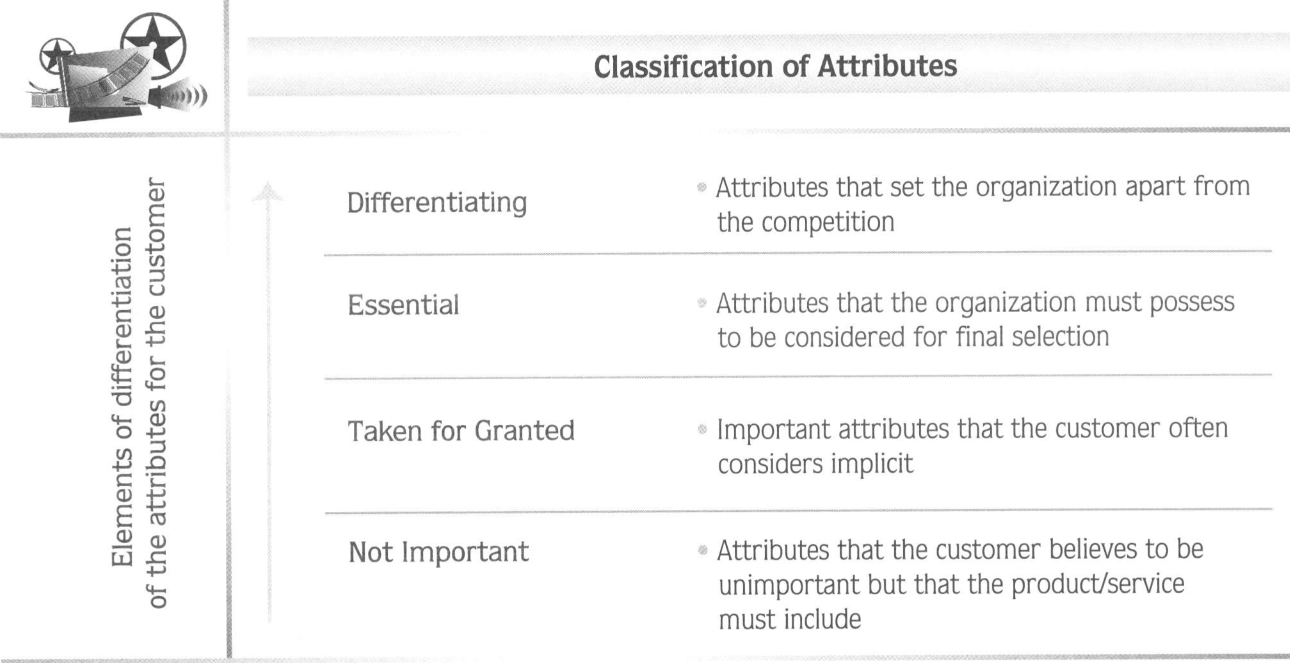

The four exercises listed on the next page will help in the understanding and classification of attributes.

Exercise 1: Attributes that set you apart

List any attributes that differentiate your organization's product/service from that of the competition.

Exercise 2: Essential attributes

List any attributes that your organization's product/service must have.

Exercise 3: Taken for granted

List any key attributes that the customer often considers to be implicit in your organization's product/service.

Exercise 4: Not important

List any attributes that the customer considers unimportant but that the product/service must include.

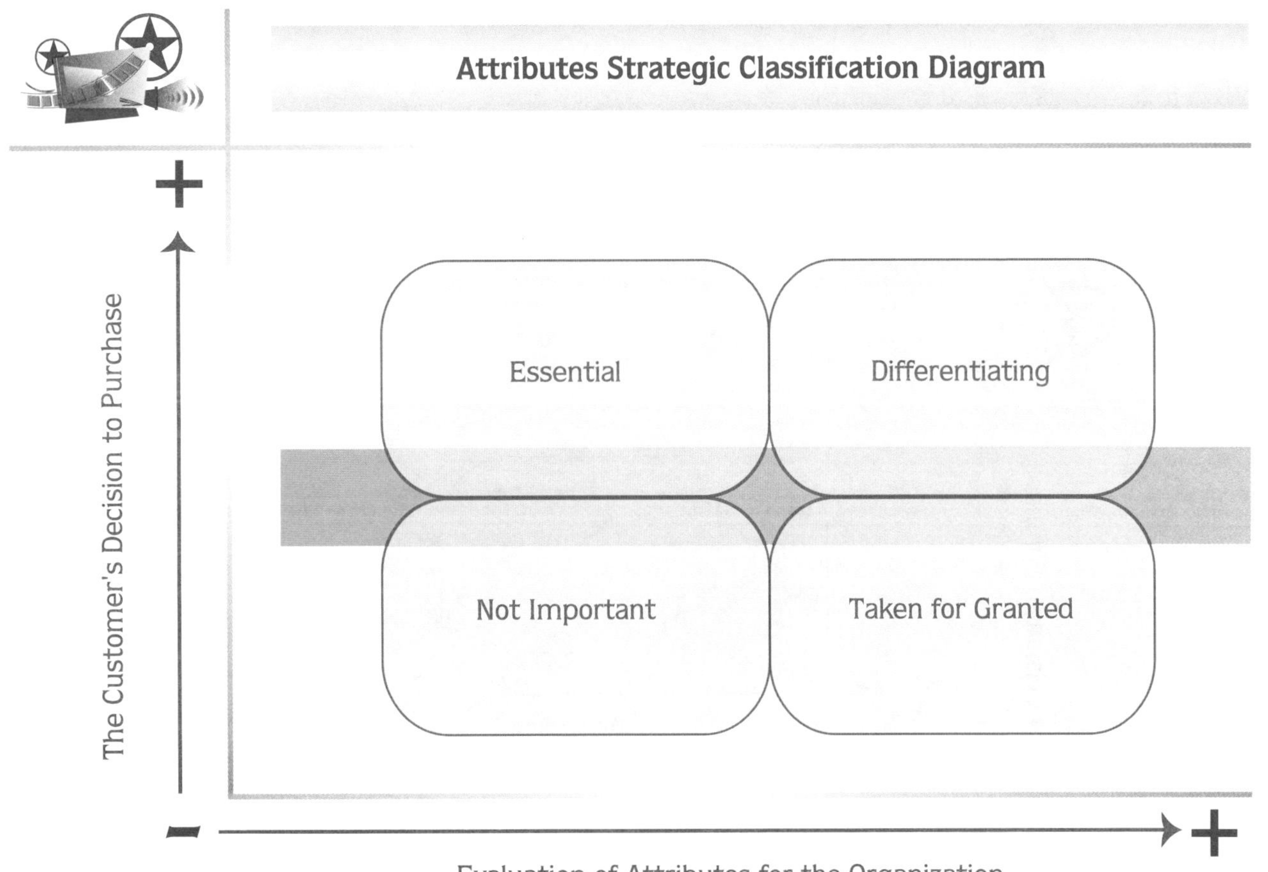
Attributes Strategic Classification Diagram
+
The Customer's Decision to Purchase
Essential
Differentiating
Not Important
Taken for Granted
–
+
Evaluation of Attributes for the Organization

The strategic classification diagram of attributes is intended to:

- Introduce, at the beginning of the customer-satisfaction survey process, some common terminology for all the organization's staff members who take part in the attributes identification.
- Serve as a point of comparison to the results of customer-satisfaction surveys in which the customer is asked to rank attributes by importance.
- Help the organization set priorities in effecting improvements.

At right is an example of a strategic classification diagram of attributes for a mechanical repair shop.

3. Construction of a Customer Satisfaction Tree

The product/service attributes identified in the strategic classification diagram can then be arranged into a customer satisfaction tree.

A customer satisfaction tree is a set of attributes pertinent to a product/service to which the customer declares his/her level of satisfaction. These attributes are then analyzed by the variance between expected quality and perceived quality (see chapter 2 for details).

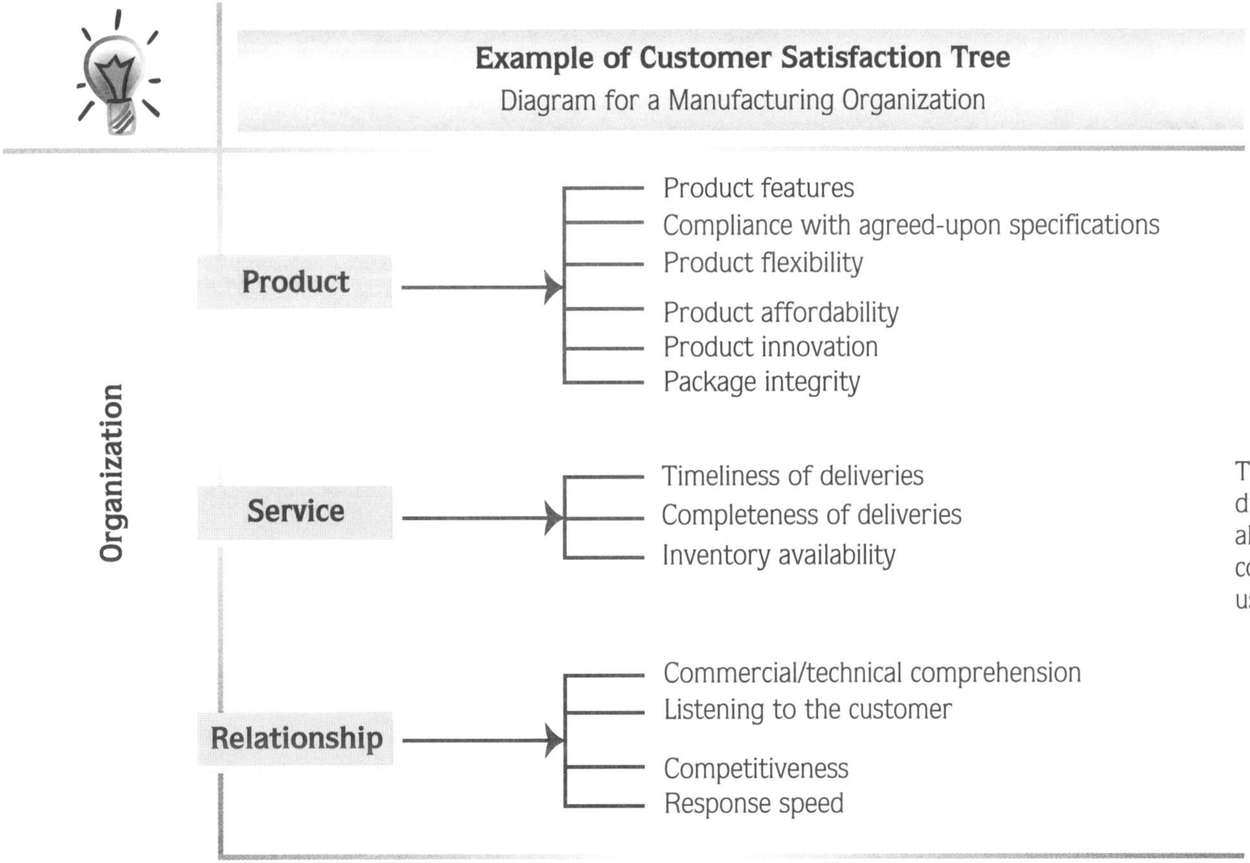

Example of Customer Satisfaction Tree

Diagram for a Manufacturing Organization

Organization

- **Product**
  - Product features
  - Compliance with agreed-upon specifications
  - Product flexibility
  - Product affordability
  - Product innovation
  - Package integrity
- **Service**
  - Timeliness of deliveries
  - Completeness of deliveries
  - Inventory availability
- **Relationship**
  - Commercial/technical comprehension
  - Listening to the customer
  - Competitiveness
  - Response speed

The satisfaction tree diagram, illustrated at left, allows an organization to construct the questionnaire used in the survey.

4. Construction of the Questionnaire

The questionnaire should ask the customer to rank the level of importance and satisfaction he/she assigns to each attribute of the organization's products/services. If possible, it should also ask the customer to compare these results to the rankings he/she would give to products/services from the organization's biggest competitor. The questionnaire should include open questions about the following points:

- Requests for hints and tips
- Overall satisfaction level
- Loyalty to the organization's products/services
- Amount of positive word-of-mouth publicity about the organization's products/services the customer gives to acquaintances

The questionnaire must initiate a dialogue with the customer based on psychological aspects such as mutual trust, esteem, goal sharing, credibility, involvement, and alignment.

The satisfaction tree diagram provides assistance in understanding WHAT the organization should ask the customer; the HOW requires further thought. The questionnaire is a communication tool between the customer and the organization. The question/answer process is comprised of four phases:

1. The organization drafts a question.
2. The customer understands the question.
3. The customer provides responses.
4. The organization records responses.

The method used in drafting questions (phase 1) is crucial to the accomplishment of reliable results. An organization must therefore adopt adequate terminology and formulate questions clearly.

Question comprehension (phase 2) is strongly linked to the previous activity: It is the first step the customer undertakes when responding to questions, and therefore it is important to the continuation of the investigation process.

During phase 3, the customer draws up a potential response. This phase begins with the customer's retrieval from memory of the necessary data and the decision he/she makes regarding the type and quantity of information required. The customer then formulates a response after an appropriate evaluation, which leads to phase 4.

Many factors can influence a customer's response; these include the desire for a return response, consistency with prior responses, and the appropriateness of survey goals.

Factors related to context can influence the degree of questionnaire completion. These include the presence of other subjects in the room, the interviewer's attitude and characteristics, and the questionnaire's graphic design.

The time and effort required to record responses vary, depending on the type of questions asked. Obviously, open questions entail a more complex recording process than closed questions. The drafters of the questionnaire, therefore, must make careful choices regarding the use of open or closed questions. The more the information required to answer a question seems remote or not important to the customer, the more likely his/her reply will be inaccurate or "I don't know."

A Sample Customer Satisfaction Questionnaire

The purpose of this questionnaire is to measure the level of product/service quality provided by [insert the name of your organization here]. Your answers will help us implement, via our quality-improvement process, our plans for improvements concerning the aspects that you believe to be most important for your success.

Instructions for completion:
Please provide your opinion on the importance of, and the degree of satisfaction you place on, the listed attributes by using a scale of 0 to 5, where 0 stands for "not important/low satisfaction" and 5 stands for "very important/high satisfaction."

Company name ______________________________

Address ______________________________

Phone ______________________________

Fax ______________________________ Date: ______________

E-mail address ______________________________

Person Interviewed:

Last name ______________________________

First Name ______________________________

Type of product purchased ______________________________

Please complete both the importance and satisfaction columns.

	Importance						Satisfaction					
1: PRODUCT												
1.1 Product features	5	4	3	2	1	0	5	4	3	2	1	0
1.2 Compliance with agreed-upon specifications	5	4	3	2	1	0	5	4	3	2	1	0
1.3 Product reliability	5	4	3	2	1	0	5	4	3	2	1	0
1.4 Product flexibility	5	4	3	2	1	0	5	4	3	2	1	0
1.5 Product innovation	5	4	3	2	1	0	5	4	3	2	1	0
1.6 Package integrity	5	4	3	2	1	0	5	4	3	2	1	0
2: SERVICE												
2.1 Completeness of deliveries	5	4	3	2	1	0	5	4	3	2	1	0
2.2 Timeliness of deliveries	5	4	3	2	1	0	5	4	3	2	1	0
2.3 Inventory availability	5	4	3	2	1	0	5	4	3	2	1	0
3: RELATIONSHIP												
3.1 Commercial/technical comprehension	5	4	3	2	1	0	5	4	3	2	1	0
3.2 Customer service	5	4	3	2	1	0	5	4	3	2	1	0
3.3 Competitiveness	5	4	3	2	1	0	5	4	3	2	1	0
3.4 Response speed	5	4	3	2	1	0	5	4	3	2	1	0
4: OVERALL SATISFACTION WITH OUR CORPORATION							5	4	3	2	1	0

overall satisfaction

5: OTHER COMMENTS

open questions

5.1 Concerning the items mentioned above ______________________________

5.2 Pertaining to your specific preferences ______________________________

loyalty

6: Will you purchase from our corporation in the future? ☐ yes ☐ no

word-of-mouth publicity

7: Would you recommend our products/services to members of other organizations? ☐ yes ☐ no

Thank-you for your time and effort in completing our survey. We will notify you of the results.

Considerations Regarding the Evaluation Scale

The scale of 0 to 5 in the sample questionnaire on the previous page permits the exclusion of a central value (if we had used a 1-to-5 scale, for example, 3 would be the median value). This might be subject to differing interpretations.

An evaluation scale ranging from 1 to 10 would allow an organization to manage its performance-improvement process step by step, but it should be used only if the customers would readily accept it.

In any event, we suggest avoiding a lengthy list of attributes for the customer's evaluation. Also to be avoided is the practice of always using the same value scales. This could generate a "response effect" whereby, after answering the initial questions, the respondent develops the attitude of assigning the same evaluation to all the other questions, regardless of their contents.

We suggest changing the questionnaire pattern by introducing open questions or additional closed questions posed in a different manner. Some surveys illustrate the meaning of every score in the evaluation scale. To be more precise in our sample questionnaire, we could have added a definition of the degree of importance/satisfaction for each level of the scale, as illustrated at right.

EXAMPLE:

IMPORTANCE

- 5 Extremely important
- 4 Very important
- 3 Somewhat important
- 2 Minimally important
- 1 Neutral
- 0 Not at all important

SATISFACTION

- 5 Extremely satisfied
- 4 Satisfied
- 3 Meets expectations
- 2 Below expectations
- 1 Poor quality
- 0 Unacceptable

The numerical scale that provides definitions only for the highest and lowest values (like the one in our sample questionnaire on the previous page) gives the customer more freedom to subjectively decide where to position responses on the scale.

On the other hand, a scale like the one above, which gives a precise definition to every score, is easier for the customer to understand and enables the organization to interpret the results simpler and faster. A disadvantage, however, is that all aspects subject to evaluation become simple qualitative variables.

5. Sampling

Good sampling depends on several factors that must be carefully assessed during the survey-design process. These factors include:

- Total number of customers receiving the questionnaire.
- An estimated percentage of questionnaires that will be completed (based on an estimate of customers' willingness to cooperate by participating in initiatives to improve products/services).
- The organization's goals in terms of accuracy of survey results and precision in execution of the questionnaire.

Ideas for Customer Segmentation
(As suggested by business managers)

- Customer importance (by profit)
- Customer business opportunities for the company
- Customer size (big and small businesses)
- Top management customers
- Agent customers
- Vendor customers
- OEM and/or manufacturing customers
- Distribution
- All customers
- Final customers
- Geographical areas (international, U.S., regional)

Identifying an appropriate sample size depends on the organization's answers to these questions: (a) What is our customer population, and how can we segment it? (b) What are our objectives with respect to our customers? Regarding question (a), we believe a preliminary analysis of the customer population is essential. An organization can divide its customer population into two or three groups based on the amount of profit they generate for the organization, by the size of customers' corporations or their geographic locations, or other segmentation criteria (listed in the box at left).

Regarding question (b), below are two sample goals that an organization might want to attain:

- Confirm the loyalty of existing customers.
- Develop potential customers.

Note that the ideal sample size normally includes about 80 to 100 customers (except for specific circumstances). This size allows an organization to stabilize its estimates on percentage values and keep expenses associated with the survey within acceptable limits.

If more than one segment must be analyzed, the overall size of the sample should be larger. For the example above, it would be preferable to create two parallel samples, each consisting of roughly 80 to 100 cases: about 100 existing customers and about 100 high-potential customers. This is because the final analysis is conducted on the two samples separately. In fact, it is likely that the aspects for improvement for existing customers will be different than those for high-potential customers.

Sampling is not necessary for organizations with a small number of customers (between 100 and 200). When the number of customers is this small, it is better to use a census instead of a survey sample. With a census, the questionnaire is mailed to all customers. Those questionnaires that are returned are analyzed, regardless of how many customers respond. The results achieved by this method are assumed to provide an accurate representation of the entire customer population.

NOTES:

6. Questionnaire Mailing and Data Collection

Before creating the final draft of its questionnaire, an organization should validate the contents by testing it on a few willing customers with whom the organization shares mutual trust. By conducting such a test, the organization accomplishes the following:

- It ensures that all activities that are important to its customers are analyzed—and, therefore, the questionnaire is complete.
- It verifies whether the questionnaire satisfies customer expectations.
- It knows whether each question is clear and understandable.

For a questionnaire to be an effective general survey tool, the return rate should be high and in line with the response percentage the organization expects. Questionnaires can be sent to customers by several methods:

- Ordinary mail (addressed by name to the quality manager where possible, or else to the most pertinent functional manager).
- Via e-mail.
- They can be completed during a visit conducted by one of the organization's staff members.

If the questionnaire is sent by mail, the organization can use specific initiatives to encourage responses, such as the following:

- A postage-paid return envelope included with the questionnaire.
- It can provide funding to not-for-profit organizations for each completed questionnaire returned.

Sending questionnaires via e-mail is the easiest and fastest method, although it can be difficult to obtain the e-mail addresses of corporate customer contacts. The letter accompanying the questionnaire must be brief and should inform the customer of the time required to complete the questionnaire (no more than fifteen minutes). Questionnaire responses should never be solicited more than twice.

Completing questionnaires during customer visits can prove to be a more expensive means than ordinary mailing or e-mailing. Furthermore, a customer might be unwilling to respond to a questionnaire during visits, preferring instead for his/her responses to be anonymous.

Scorecards

A Useful Tool for Top Management Customers or Strategic Customers

Scorecards are preferable for important or strategic customers, since they require substantial time and effort on the part of both the customer and the organization. This type of survey is conducted using indicators or parameters previously identified by the customer and the organization pertaining to the following:

- Gauging schedules (e.g., monthly, quarterly, or for the duration of an existing contract).
- Evaluation scale (we suggest using scales with which the customer is already familiar, such as 0–5 or 1–10).
- Value attributes for the customer (e.g., delivery flexibility or order completeness).

The customer defines the attributes, so the number of possible scorecards equals the number of customers who agree to use this tool.

How to Proceed?

With important or strategic customers, the organization and the customer decide together what aspects to monitor, the evaluation scale to adopt, and the meeting schedule. Everything is reported in a file that is analyzed by both the customer and the organization before each scheduled meeting.

Both the customer and the organization provide evaluations of attributes. The customer evaluates the product or service he/she receives, and the organization evaluates the product or service it provides. Any variance resulting from such evaluations must be accounted for by the organization.

The organization then implements any actions it deems necessary to improve its performance. The results are discussed in future meetings with the customer.

Evaluation of attributes by both the customer and the organization, using a scale from 1 to 10.

A Sample Scorecard

First-Level Attributes	Second-Level Attributes	Customer	Organization	Variance
Product	Product Features	8	9	-1
	Compliance with Specifications	8	8	0
Service	Timeliness of Deliveries	8	7	+1
	Completeness of Deliveries	9	7	+2
Relationship	Response Speed	6	8	-2

Calculation of variance between the two standpoints

Scorecard Strengths

- This tool generates a lot of positive interaction and relationship between the organization and the customer.
- The organization creates a product/service that satisfies the customer's implied needs.
- The business manager can take advantage of any opportunities that might arise during contract execution with the customer.
- The organization can immediately implement any necessary corrective or preventive actions.
- The organization can translate suggestions stemming from customized customer relationships into overall improvement of the products/services it offers to all its customers.
- Staff members of both the customer and the organization become involved in the implementation of activities that are pertinent to the attributes evaluated in the scorecard.

Scorecard Weaknesses

- When a customer is dissatisfied, the organization might be unable to immediately respond to other customer requests due to a lack of resources (or due to other reasons).
- Measurements that are frequent or that bear results that are constantly aligned by both parties might instill disbelief in the cost/benefit relationship of those measurements.

Response Cards

Response cards are particularly useful for surveys that measure the customer's perception about the products and services he/she receives. They allow for an immediate performance evaluation, since the judgment is rendered at the time of product delivery or service provision. The card is completed by the end-user of the product or service.

> Example: For a clothes-cleaning service, the supplier delivers clean garments along with a preprinted response card and asks the customer to complete it and send it back to the company. The card can include questions about service provision, auxiliary services (e.g., packaging or clothing scent), and overall customer satisfaction.

This tool is straightforward to use and requires the organization to react according to the results. Negative scores require additional contact with the customer to better understand the reasons for dissatisfaction and to make efforts to find causes and begin appropriate corrective action. Positive scores should be analyzed so the same results happen with all customers in the future.

Response cards should be duly disseminated to all of an organization's customers and stress the organization's efforts to meet their needs. The results of these analyses should be recorded and filed in appropriate databases that allow the data to be represented in different ways and to be parsed by service, customer segment, or personnel involved in implementation. The resulting analyses should provide top management with information concerning any problems with product/service implementation processes, with perception of some customers' needs, or any lack of skills or training among the organization's staff.

Strength: The end user can be reached through vendors or distributors, since the cards can be included in product packaging.

Weakness: Organizations that use this tool report that the customer response rate is often low.

Complaint Management

Research conducted by the American Management Association reveals that only about 4% of dissatisfied customers express their disappointment to the organization, especially if the complaint procedures are complicated and perceived as useless. Complaint management is an important activity even though it might not be useful for detecting general customer satisfaction or dissatisfaction, considering the small number of complaints compared to the number of customers.

Effective complaint management can lead to new information. In many instances it can actually be fundamental in keeping customers because, although they are dissatisfied, they might appreciate that the organization pays attention to their complaints. Thus, complaint management is actually an opportunity for improving customer loyalty.

Complaint analysis must be structured. In-depth inquiries should reveal the most recurring causes for complaints. The organization must pay careful attention to each cause in terms of three factors:

- time needed to resolve the complaint
- customer importance
- problem severity

NOTE: The SDA Bocconi 2000 research conducted on a group of small businesses affiliated with the Quality Consortium revealed that one of the weaknesses in complaint management was the lack of a severity code (see chapter 4).

Once a complaint occurs, after the organization classifies and files all the related data, the managers of the department responsible for the nonconformity should immediately start any required corrective and/or preventive actions. Once the complaint-resolution process is over, the organization should verify and measure the effectiveness over time of the actions taken.

Based on the continuous-process-improvement principle of corporate quality systems, the process of complaint resolution should constantly improve. Therefore, it is essential that the organization periodically (e.g., monthly) produce reports on its management of complaints, indicating the best and worst departments or functions. This raises the awareness of customer complaints and needs throughout the entire organization.

Strengths

- This method allows the organization to attempt to recoup the complaining customer's satisfaction. A complaint can be turned into an opportunity for increasing customer loyalty.
- Complaint recording is required by the ISO standards.
- Complaints can confirm other dissatisfaction data that the organization receives from customer surveys.
- The nature of the complaints received through this method and their resolution might prevent further dissatisfaction or complaints from other customers.

Weaknesses

- Complaint management involves "reactive quality"; it normally begins only after the problem has taken place.
- This method is a customer listening tool oriented toward only the customer's basic needs (see chapter 2).

Visits to Customers

Customer visits offer an organization a great opportunity to systematically collect its customers' perceptions about its products/services. A structured and continuous information-collection process associated with these visits allows the organization to validate or analyze the results of customer surveys it conducts by different means.

Strengths

- Customer perceptions regarding the products/services provided are carefully recorded.
- This method gives an organization the opportunity to reinforce its relationship with its customers.

Weaknesses

- Customer perceptions are often qualitative rather than quantitative.
- It is difficult to standardize the recording of visit results and, consequently, to effect an objective analysis.

Follow-Up Telephone Calls

An organization can conduct a follow-up phone call to a customer for several reasons after a complaint: to ensure the complaint has been resolved within the scheduled timing, to confirm that some or all of the customer's suggestions were implemented, or to inquire into causes for dissatisfaction following negative responses on surveys.

The purpose of the follow-up telephone call is to further reinforce a customer relationship after a specific event occurs. However, follow-up phone calls are NOT meant to acquire additional orders from a customer or to propose new solutions to a problem.

Strengths

- This method reinforces the relationship between the customer and the organization through dialogue and communication.
- This method demonstrates an organization's consideration for all its customers.

Weakness

- Too much consideration on the part of the organization can be cause for rejection by the customer or can give the false impression that the organization spends more time and effort on customer care than it does on improving the quality of its products/services.

Intermediate Monitoring

An organization's commitment plan for its customers should consider intermediate monitoring of all the activities the business manager is to implement over a predefined time span. (This is also called an intermediate survey; see the customer satisfaction implementation model [step B] described in chapter 5.)

Intermediate monitoring often consists of a mini-questionnaire requesting the customer's opinion of a maximum of five or six attributes. This is conducted with a limited number of customers over the phone.

The primary goal of intermediate monitoring is to ensure that an organization's improvement activities are producing the expected results. Most important, it allows the organization to understand whether it is on the right path or whether it needs to enact changes to its current plans or objectives.

Strengths

- Intermediate monitoring can be conducted by the organization's staff members.
- This method requires only a small time commitment, due to the limited numbers of attributes being evaluated and customers being interviewed.
- The telephone contact done during this method confirms the organization's commitment to its customers.

Weakness

- Because it is not an extensive survey and is based on a restricted customer sample, intermediate monitoring provides limited information and can only confirm existing trends.

A Sample Script and Questions for Intermediate Monitoring of Customer Satisfaction

During the telephone interview, use the following script when addressing the customer: "We are verifying that our quality-improvement process is producing the expected results. Could you please answer the following five questions? This will not take up more than two minutes of your time. For each question, please assign a score from 0 to 5, where 0 means 'low satisfaction' and 5 means 'high satisfaction.'"

	Satisfaction					
1: PRODUCT						
1.3 Product reliability	5	4	3	2	1	0
1.4 Compliance with agreed-upon specifications	5	4	3	2	1	0
2: SERVICE						
1.3 Product reliability	5	4	3	2	1	0
3: RELATIONSHIP						
3.2 Customer listening	5	4	3	2	1	0
4: OVERALL SATISFACTION	5	4	3	2	1	0

Chapter Seven

The Commitment Plan

- Progressing from mere knowledge of the tools to creating targeted planning for your own market

Legend

Concept Projection

Explanation/Advice

Exercise

Example

Web-Site Reference
www.goalqpc.com/customer

Planning

An effective plan of activities for customer-satisfaction measurement and improvement should include the following steps.

1. Focus and agree on the goals to pursue in terms of customer satisfaction. Share these goals throughout the organization.
2. Select the most appropriate tools for accomplishing these goals.
3. Set up a schedule for the implementation of activities.
4. Identify resources to deploy in the process.
5. Quantify the costs required to achieve the defined goals.

Following these steps results in a commitment plan regarding the customer, including the identification of the most appropriate survey tools (see the customer satisfaction survey model [step A] in chapter 5).

Survey Commitment Plan for the Customer

Yearly scheduling of activities allows for savings and results optimization

	Jan.	Feb.	Mar.	April	May	June	July	Aug.	Sept.	Oct.	Nov.	Dec.	Suggested Frequency
Survey Techniques													
General survey (▲) by means of questionnaire													Once a year
Customer Interface Techniques													
Visit to customer (▲)													Constant
Complaint management (▲)													Constant
Performance-Monitoring Tools													
Response cards (■)													Based on product/service
Follow-up phone calls (■)													Every 3–4 months
Intermediate monitoring (▲)													One or more times a year
Scorecards (▲)													Every 6 months

Strongly recommended (▲) Recommended (■)

Chapter 6 outlines the appropriate tools an organization can use for creating a customer satisfaction survey, as well as the specific goals of using each tool. Once the specific goals of a customer satisfaction survey are clear, the organization can select a planning tool that will best help it to meet those goals. The survey commitment plan for the customer, shown on the previous page, serves this purpose.

The left column of the chart shows the survey techniques and performance-monitoring tools that an organization can adopt to improve customer relations and to collect information. The techniques and tools are divided into three categories:

- General survey
- Customer interface (i.e., visits to customers, complaint management)
- Performance-monitoring techniques (i.e., response cards, follow-up phone calls, intermediate monitoring, scorecards)

The right side of the chart shows a suggested frequency of use for these tools. An organization should determine this frequency according to the type of product or service it provides. In planning the use of survey techniques, the organization should take care to consider the needs of its customers and not annoy them with excessive questionnaires and surveys.

In-depth general surveys are normally conducted only once a year. Their frequency is based on the abilities of the internal staff members who collect and process the data, taking into account the amount of time they have to spend attending meetings and planning improvement activities.

Finally, an organization's choice of tools should take into account the cost implications of the survey process—mailing the survey, soliciting feedback, data entry, and the statistical processing of results. This helps the organization to assess the resources available and to determine any additional resources that it needs to perform these activities.

Chapter Eight
The Analysis

What results can be achieved through customer satisfaction surveys? Appropriate processing of data collected through survey tools can help in assessing a customer's:

- priorities (attributes-importance status)
- performance evaluation (satisfaction status)
- performance evaluation of the organization's best competitor, if possible (competitive status)

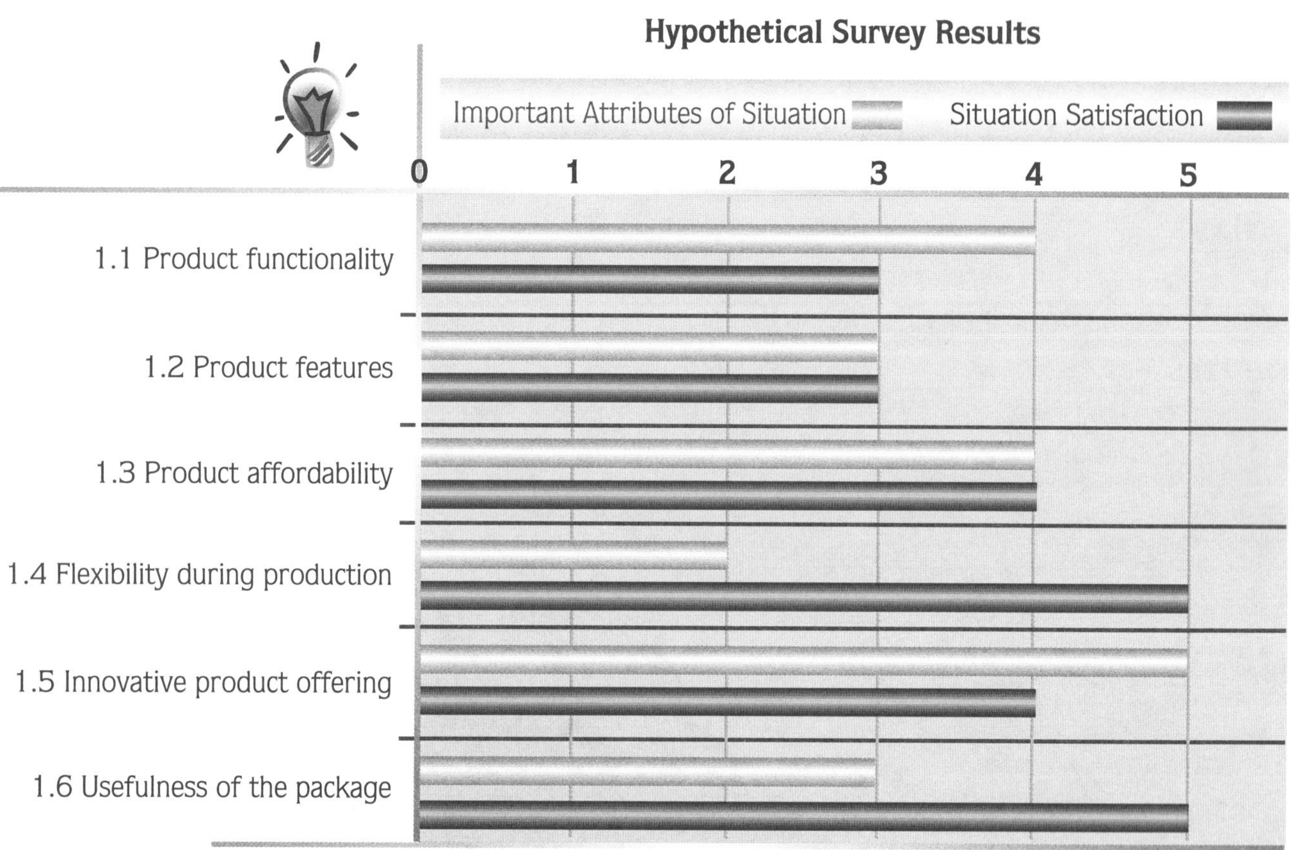
Hypothetical Survey Results
Important Attributes of Situation
Situation Satisfaction
0
1
2
3
4
5
1.1 Product functionality
1.2 Product features
1.3 Product affordability
1.4 Flexibility during production
1.5 Innovative product offering
1.6 Usefulness of the package

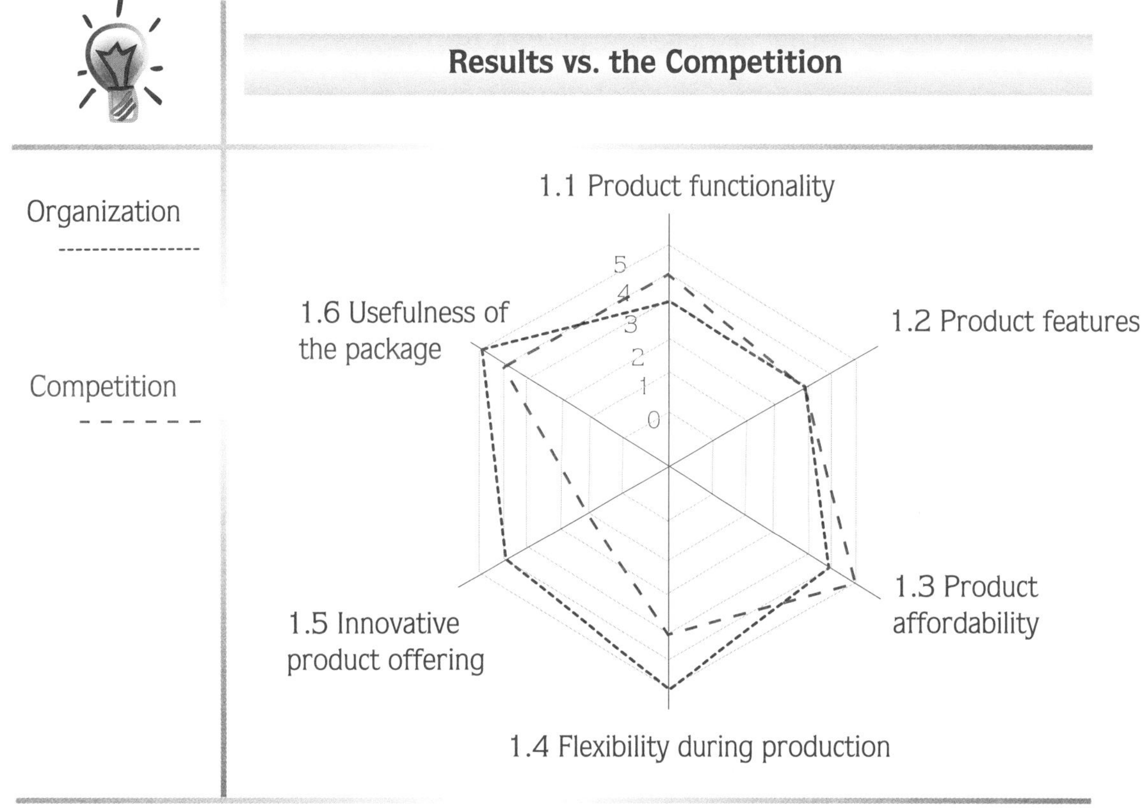
Results vs. the Competition
Organization
Competition
1.1 Product functionality
1.2 Product features
1.3 Product affordability
1.4 Flexibility during production
1.5 Innovative product offering
1.6 Usefulness of the package
5
4
3
2
1
0

Importance/Satisfaction Diagram

	Low Satisfaction	High Satisfaction	
High Importance	**Primary Critical Area** Low Satisfaction/ High Importance Problem areas ↓ Improvement opportunities	**Primary Maintenance Area** High Satisfaction/ High Importance Satisfaction strengths	5
Low Importance	**Secondary Critical Area** Low Satisfaction/ Low Importance Dissatisfaction factors	**Secondary Maintenance Area** High Satisfaction/ Low Importance The efforts invested are not always necessary	2.5

Importance (vertical axis)

Low ← Satisfaction → High

Analysis

It's important to use the proper metrics to analyze customer satisfaction/ importance results gathered from surveys. The business manager of a small or medium-size firm needs to use indicators, especially when carrying out customer satisfaction surveys for the first time, that allow decision-making based on facts rather than on opinion.

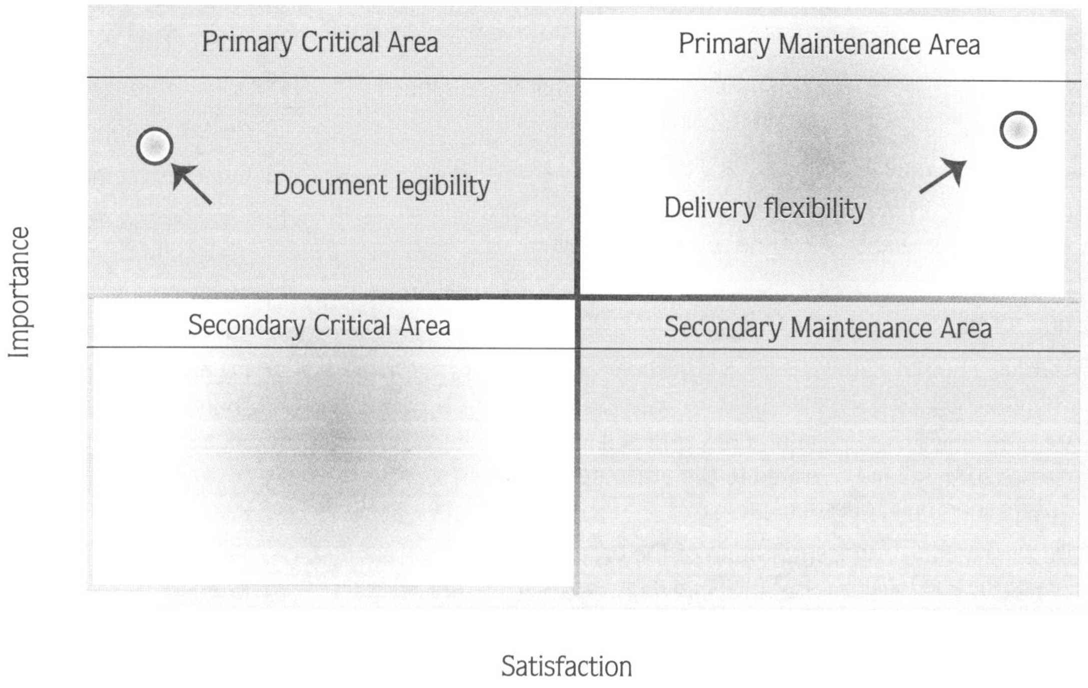

The results of customer surveys can be quickly analyzed by using the diagram shown at right. The horizontal axis shows satisfaction, while the vertical axis shows importance.

Primary Critical Area
Document legibility
Primary Maintenance Area
Delivery flexibility
Importance
Secondary Critical Area
Secondary Maintenance Area
Satisfaction

The evaluation scale should be similar to the one used for customers' responses. (We adopted a 0-to-5 scale for the case studies shown in chapter 10.) Attributes evaluations are inserted into the appropriate boxes. For instance, in the diagram at right, because a customer gave "delivery flexibility" a satisfaction score of 5 and an importance score of 5, it has been placed in the "Primary Maintenance Area" portion of the diagram. "Document legibility" was given a satisfaction score of 2 and an importance score of 4, so it has been placed in the "Primary Critical Area" portion of the diagram.

Once all customer evaluations are placed in the diagram, the results can be compared to those from the initial self-evaluation exercise (see chapter 4) and those from the strategic classification of customer value attributes (see chapter 6).

Any variance that is observed in such comparisons stems from the different perceptions that the business manager and other staff members might have regarding customer perceptions about the different attributes being reviewed.

Use the following questions as a checklist for making decisions regarding survey results:

- ❑ Is the data collected consistent with the goals that were defined at the beginning of the process? (scope and action plan)
- ❑ Was enough time allotted for data collection? (scheduling)
- ❑ Does the return rate for questionnaires or return cards allow for an adequate analysis of the results? (sampling)
- ❑ Did all customers express their level of importance and satisfaction for all listed attributes? (survey completeness)
- ❑ Have all "Do not know" responses been considered? (clearness and understanding of questions)
- ❑ Were responses to open questions grouped into homogeneous classes so they can be related to the attributes? (difficulties in interpreting open questions)
- ❑ Do the results allow identification of the organization's strengths and weaknesses? (use of simple diagrams or charts)
- ❑ Did any substantial market changes occur between the time the survey was conducted and the time the results were collected? (new competitors, innovative products/services)

Further analysis should include information from the following sources. This will enable the organization to better address the business manager's efforts:

- ❑ Customer appreciation letters.
- ❑ Customer complaints.
- ❑ Internal and external audit results, such as the ISO Standard inspection.
- ❑ Evaluation or self-evaluation results for various types of acknowledgments, such as the Malcolm Baldrige National Quality Award.
- ❑ Feedback from customer-contact staff, customer-assistance personnel, and sales officers, plus feedback from internal customers regarding comments received from external customers.
- ❑ Comparisons with organizations generally acknowledged as the best in the market due to their efficiency and the effectiveness of their processes.
- ❑ Number of customers acquired and lost during the time span under investigation.

From Analysis to Action

Not all improvements or changes stemming from data analysis can be implemented immediately.

The first step an organization should take in the implementation process is to involve staff members from the beginning when deciding which improvements or change plans to select. The speed of the implementation can be increased only by sharing goals and by gaining everyone's approval up front. Improvement activities are easier if staff members participate in the identification of customer satisfaction attributes and in the collection of information required to determine priority areas.

The next step is to draft an improvement plan. A working group, with its own specific goals, should be created for every project and every area for which improvement processes have been identified. Each group should complete the following tasks:

- ❑ Implement new metrics and collect and analyze data.
- ❑ Implement preventive and/or corrective change actions.
- ❑ Check to see that established goals have been achieved.
- ❑ Maintain accomplished improvements.
- ❑ Identify new improvement projects.

The improvement methodology that we recommend using is the PDCA Cycle (or "Deming Cycle," as it is often called), where

P	stands for	Plan
D	stands for	Do
C	stands for	Check
A	stands for	Act

When implementing the fundamental principles, management criteria, and the methodologies and techniques for quality improvement, it is a good idea to consult the ISO 9004:2000 Quality Management Systems Guidelines for Performance Improvement.

Legend

Concept Projection

Explanation/Advice

Exercise

Example

Web-Site Reference
www.goalqpc.com/customer

Chapter Nine

The Traps

- Errors to avoid
- Avoiding pitfalls and common mistakes made during the customer satisfaction improvement process

What Are the Traps Involved in Measuring Customer Satisfaction and Implementing Improvements?

These traps fall into two major areas, as described below.

Management Area

1. Not using customer satisfaction survey results and basing business decisions on guesswork rather than on metrics.
2. Restricting the dissemination of customers' opinions within the organization.
3. Disregarding the improvement speed of the organization's main competition.
4. Not meeting customers' expectations after creating them.

Technical Area and/or Related Tools

1. Using partial data and/or insignificant samples.
2. Using tools that are either too sophisticated or ineffective.
3. Having difficulty processing customer responses to open questions.
4. Performing too many analyses and very few actions.
5. Spending too much time on "measuring the past."

Management-Area Traps

1. NOT USING CUSTOMER SATISFACTION SURVEY RESULTS AND BASING BUSINESS DECISIONS ON GUESSWORK RATHER THAN ON METRICS

This is one of the most common management traps. Two typical situations that a business manager might confront proceed as follows:

A. The analysis results meet his/her expectations for customer-satisfaction level. The manager then asks, "The analysis revealed nothing I didn't already know; did we need to invest all this time and effort?"

B. When results do not match expectations, defense mechanisms might come into play. If results are negative, the business manager might say, "it just wasn't the right time to conduct a survey" or "there must be a mistake." If results are overwhelmingly positive, the manager might say, "everything is fine as it is; we couldn't do any better."

These attitudes do not permit an in-depth understanding of the survey, since they do not let the organization get a feeling for the data. In these cases, most likely the organization will continue to operate as it has in the past without enacting any changes based on customer results.

2. RESTRICTING THE DISSEMINATION OF CUSTOMERS' OPINIONS WITHIN THE ORGANIZATION

This is a cultural trap that derives from mission, vision, and quality policies. Top management's and the business manager's behavior must exhibit to everyone in the organization that the customer is of value to the organization. Implementing customer satisfaction monitoring systems without adequate staff training or customer care might result in greater frustration and dissatisfaction for everyone. The communication process whereby everyone within the organization understands the customer's perceptions about the products/services provided and what is being done for the customer must be represented in the organization's daily work. The business manager should not be the only one in the organization to know what the customer thinks and wishes; all of an organization's business structures must be in line with each other. How can the organization's staff contribute to the improvement of business processes if they are not acquainted with customers' expectations and perceptions?

3. DISREGARDING THE IMPROVEMENT SPEED OF THE ORGANIZATION'S MAIN COMPETITION

In today's globally competitive environment, being the leader in one's industry does not necessarily imply permanent market leadership.

An organization must understand the pace of improvement of its competition and compare itself to the best corporations in terms of operating processes, people, products/services, innovation, and actions taken to make daily improvements.

An organization must remain humble even when it is at the top of its field. High-sounding attitudes have caused more than one organization to subsequently disappear from the market.

4. NOT MEETING CUSTOMERS' EXPECTATIONS AFTER CREATING THEM

A customer responds to interviews, questionnaires, and so forth with the belief that he/she is dealing with an organization that actively listens to customers' needs and then takes appropriate actions to meet them.

If these remedial actions do not happen within a certain time span, the disappointed customer might gain revenge in the following ways:

Telephone surveys: He/she will not answer the phone or will always be tied up in meetings.

Visits: The customer will never have time to meet with suppliers.

Questionnaires: The trash basket becomes the customer's best friend.

Internet surveys: The "cancel" button will allow the customer to click away anything he/she finds annoying.

Technical Area and/or Related Tools

1. USING PARTIAL DATA AND/OR INSIGNIFICANT SAMPLES

This is one of the most common tool-related traps.

Despite the strict application of the methodology an organization adopts to find the correct segmentation and determine all attributes that create value for the customer, sometimes the collected data is not significantly representative of the entire customer population, or it is incomplete. Making business decisions based on such partial or incomplete data can result in risky business decisions.

2. USING TOOLS THAT ARE EITHER TOO SOPHISTICATED OR INEFFECTIVE

Customers might not always be able to comprehend sophisticated tools to assess satisfaction. As a result, scorecards, which are generally used with big or strategic customers, are not commonly used.

Customer group interviews and in-depth interviews involve the use of qualitative surveys, which sometimes require customers to divulge very sensitive information. The use of incomplete, inaccurate, or superficial surveys can result in risky business decisions.

3. HAVING DIFFICULTY PROCESSING CUSTOMER RESPONSES TO OPEN QUESTIONS

The use of multiple-choice questions or open questions that require more than a simple yes-or-no answer requires qualitative data processing. This is an analytical and comprehension effort that takes a lot of time and patience on behalf of the organization's staff members.

The organization's business manager must set clear-cut goals for analysis of these responses. Because they are sometimes unclear, they often require interpretation.

4. PERFORMING TOO MANY ANALYSES AND VERY FEW ACTIONS

Once a survey is completed, usually the organization quickly ends up with massive amounts of documentation resulting from detailed and sophisticated analyses that are not always easy to interpret.

The presentation of results should not deter from their readability. The business manager needs complete, significant, clear data that enables him/her to take appropriate and immediate action and produce results in the short term.

Most of all, he/she needs summary data that briefly and clearly identifies the organization's strengths and weaknesses so he/she can determine priority areas that call for immediate intervention.

One way to do this is to measure the number and entity of actions the organization takes following each survey and to evaluate their effectiveness in priority areas.

5. SPENDING TOO MUCH TIME ON "MEASURING THE PAST"

Although an organization can ask its customers about their perceptions of product/service quality only after they make a purchase, the business manager needs to be able to understand and affect future purchase behavior before it happens.

To avoid excessively focusing on the past, the organization can assign more weight to customer questions regarding loyalty and word-of-mouth publicity, such as the following:

Would you purchase again from our company?

Would you recommend our company to your acquaintances?

An organization should also check the number of surveys it has conducted in the past when determining how many it should conduct in the future.

Chapter Ten

Case Histories

- Practical experiences
- Experiment results
- Tools "in practice"

Experiments with Three Real-World Business Managers

These experiments involved four meetings between the authors and the business managers of three companies: Salvi S.p.A., Rentex S.p.A., and Dal Cin S.p.A. These meetings were also attended by representatives of Assolombarda and the Quality Consortium. Each of these meetings was a significant stepping-stone for these businesses on the road to measuring and winning customer satisfaction. The agenda and contents of these four meetings are shown below.

The following pages contain details about the three companies and the most significant steps they took during these experiments.

July 6, 1999	October 1, 1999	November 4, 1999		April 30, 2000
• Presentation of index to business managers • The customer's role in the evolution of ISO 9000 Standard requirements • Presentation of the customer satisfaction survey model • Analysis of customer value attributes	• Analysis of meeting held with corporate staff • Self-evaluation exercise on leadership • Construction of customer satisfaction tree diagram	• Sampling of reference customers for the general survey • Selection of survey tools • Presentation of each commitment plan to customers: 1. Creation of tool with questions for customers (questionnaire) 2. Project implementation schedule (timing and resources involved) 3. Expected survey results	January–March 2000: Surveys conducted	• Analysis of collected data and results, achieved by means of charts • Importance/satisfaction diagram • Discussion of action plans

Salvi S.p.A.

Business Description

For fifty years, Salvi S.p.A. has been in the wire business, using state-of-the-art technological materials. Its products have diverse utilizations and applications.

INDUSTRY: Wires and electrical and phone conductors

ANNUAL PROFIT: 4.3 million Euros, 50% of which comes from international activities

NUMBER OF STAFF MEMBERS: 40

"Our quality policy consists of customer satisfaction. Our test laboratories guarantee product innovation and quality control. The ISO UNI EN 29002 Standard Certification, which we obtained in 1993, ensures quality and continuous improvement of all our activities." (Source: www.salvi-spa.com)

Experimentation Method

PERSON INVOLVED: The business manager

EXPERIMENTATION STEPS:

SELF-EVALUATION ON LEADERSHIP: Salvi had a good overall average score of 7.5. The lowest score received was for point 2 (survey data is not used to define action priorities). The highest score received was for point 8 (the business manager knows well the primary reasons for the loss of some of Salvi's customers).

MEETING WITH STAFF: The business manager, together with direct colleagues and staff members, outlines the principal attributes of the Salvi commercial offer that create value for customers' businesses. The results are outlined in the diagram on the next page.

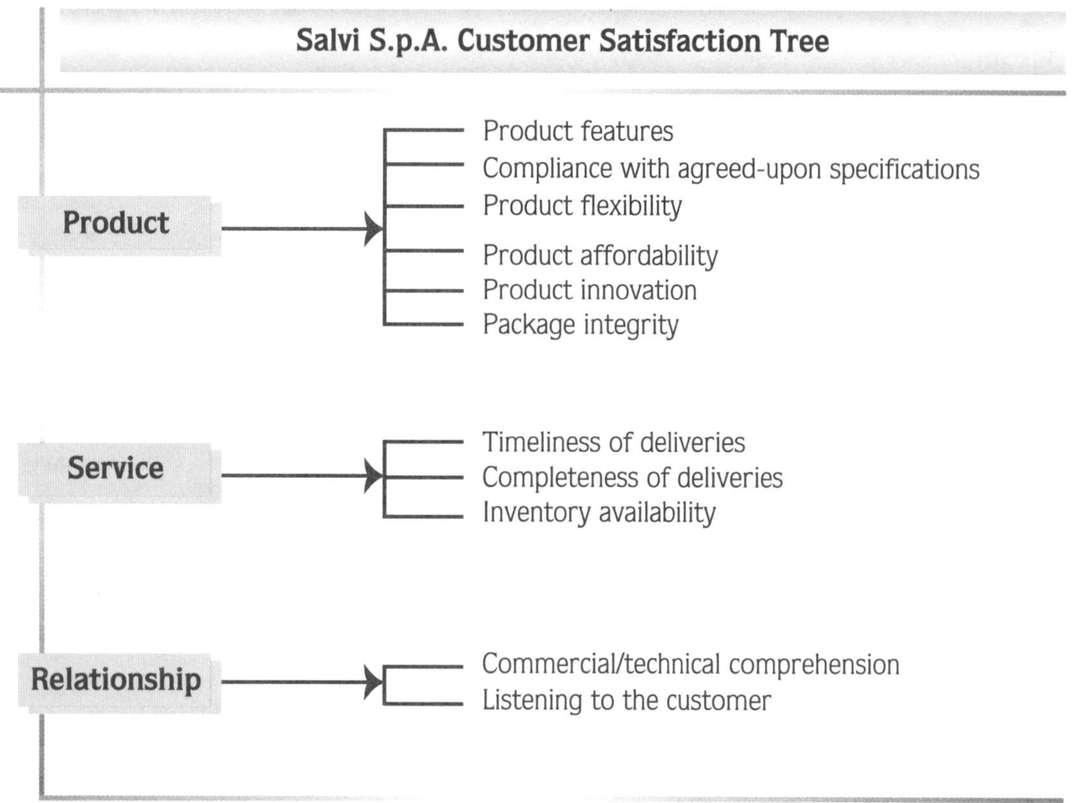

The elements for constructing this diagram were provided by Salvi's business manager and quality assurance manager, along with members of Salvi's technical and product development, sales, commercial, production, and administration divisions.

A Sample Customer Satisfaction Questionnaire

The purpose of this questionnaire is to mea
service quality provided by [insert the name
Your answers will help us implement, via
process, our plans for improvements conce
believe to be most important for your succ

Instructions for completion:
Please provide your opinion on the impor
satisfaction you place on, the listed attribut
where 0 stands for "not important/low sa
"very important/high satisfaction."

Company name ____

Address ____

Phone ____

Fax ____

E-mail address ____

Person Interviewed:

Last name ____

First Name ____

Type of product purchased ____

Please complete both the importance and satisfaction columns.

	Importance	Satisfaction
1: PRODUCT		
1.1 Product features	5 4 3 2 1 0	5 4 3 2 1 0
1.2 Compliance with agreed-upon specifications	5 4 3 2 1 0	5 4 3 2 1 0
1.3 Product reliability	5 4 3 2 1 0	5 4 3 2 1 0
1.4 Product flexibility	5 4 3 2 1 0	5 4 3 2 1 0
1.5 Product innovation	5 4 3 2 1 0	5 4 3 2 1 0
1.6 Package integrity	5 4 3 2 1 0	5 4 3 2 1 0
2: SERVICE		
2.1 Completeness of deliveries	5 4 3 2 1 0	5 4 3 2 1 0
2.2 Timeliness of deliveries	5 4 3 2 1 0	5 4 3 2 1 0
2.3 Inventory availability	5 4 3 2 1 0	5 4 3 2 1 0
3: RELATIONSHIP		
3.1 Commercial/technical comprehension	5 4 3 2 1 0	5 4 3 2 1 0
3.2 Customer service	5 4 3 2 1 0	5 4 3 2 1 0
3.3 Competitiveness	5 4 3 2 1 0	5 4 3 2 1 0
3.4 Response speed	5 4 3 2 1 0	5 4 3 2 1 0
4: OVERALL SATISFACTION WITH OUR CORPORATION		5 4 3 2 1 0

5: OTHER COMMENTS

5.1 Concerning the items mentioned above ____

5.2 Pertaining to your specific preferences ____

6: Will you purchase from our corporation in the future? ☐ yes ☐ no

7: Would you recommend our products/services to members of other organizations? ☐ yes ☐ no

Thank-you for your time and effort in completing our survey. We will notify you of the results.

Results of Customer Satisfaction Survey Conducted by Salvi S.p.A.

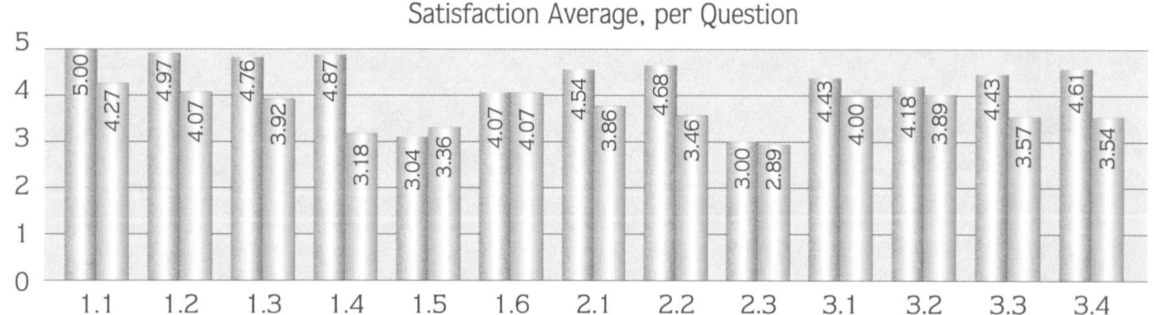

Questions
1.1 through 3.4

Satisfaction Average

Overall Satisfaction

Question 4

Comparision of Satisfaction Average and Overall Satisfaction

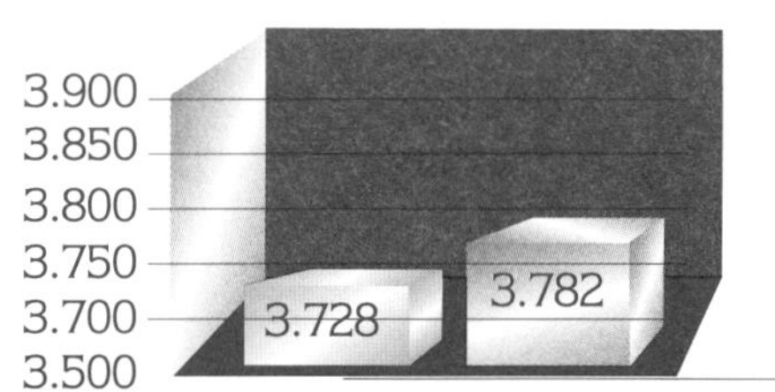

Question 6

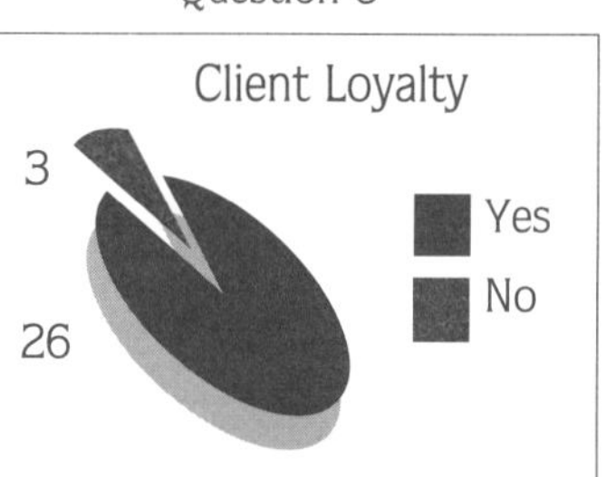

Question 7

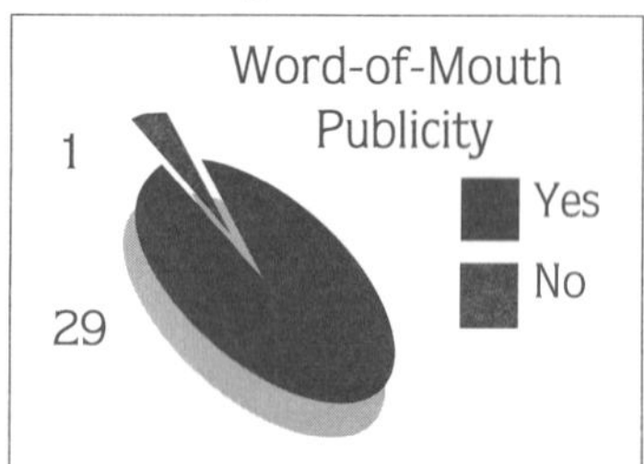

CUSTOMER SATISFACTION

Operating Plan and Data Collection

The business manager selected 54 of the 158 customers (50% of whom were foreign) to whom the survey questionnaire was submitted. In an effort to make this sample group represent the whole population, the following selection criteria were adopted: the importance of the customer in terms of profit, the location (domestic or international), and the distribution channel (manufacturing, wiring, or distribution). The response rate was higher than 50%. One-third of the customers replied spontaneously by faxing a completed questionnaire, while all others were solicited by phone.

Survey Results and Actions Taken

The review of the data from Salvi's survey focused on the importance for customers (a score of 4.7) and on the degree of satisfaction (a score of 3.5) concerning timeliness of deliveries. The actions taken by the Salvi corporation to improve the timeliness of deliveries included designing a new production planning system and, in the short term, increasing customer communication during order confirmation and execution (see the detailed plan below).

Improvement plan: critical areas for year 2000

Area	Specification	Improvement Actions	Plan	Date of Implementation
Product	Feature	Maintenance	Nonconformity test	12.30.00
Product	Specifications compliance	Maintenance	Nonconformity test	12.30.00
Product	Affordability	Maintenance	Nonconformity test	12.30.00
Product	Production flexibility	New production planning system	In studio	12.30.00
Product	Innovation of products provided	Maintenance	Customer satisfaction 2K	12.30.00
Product	Packaging integrity	Maintenance	Nonconformity test	12.30.00
Service	Completeness of deliveries	Programming of the new product	In studio	12.30.00
Service	Timeliness of deliveries	Programming of the new product	In studio	12.30.00
Service	Inventory availability	Important only for vendors	Product requirement analysis	12.30.00
Relationship	Accessibility	Improvement	Interface table	3.15.00
			Internet project	12.30.00
Relationship	Customer listening	Internet project	Interface table	3.15.00
			Internet project	
Relationship	Competitiveness	Monitor	Customer visits	Over the year
Relationship	Response speed	Improvement	Interface table	3.15.00

Rentex S.p.A.

Business Description

Since 1980, Rentex has provided customized rentals of work clothing, including washing, pickup, and delivery, along with a range of auxiliary services (e.g., mending, repair, and inventory management). These services are primarily provided to the pharmaceutical, chemical, food, and health industries.

INDUSTRY: Industrial laundry and garment rental

ANNUAL PROFIT: 7.2 million euros

NUMBER OF STAFF MEMBERS: 70

Rentex gained quality certification in December 1998 by complying with the ISO Standard 9002 requirements. The company is now preparing to obtain the ISO 14000 Standard Environmental Certification. (Source: www.rentex.it)

Experimentation Method

PERSON INVOLVED: The business manager

EXPERIMENTATION STEPS:

SELF-EVALUATION ON LEADERSHIP: Rentex had a good overall average score of 8.2. The lowest scores received were for points 1 and 2 (Rentex does not conduct surveys to monitor customer satisfaction); the highest scores received were for points 6 through 10 (corporate staff know their strategic customers well and are informed of all successful actions with respect to their customers).

MEETING WITH STAFF: The business manager did not pay attention to the customer satisfaction surveys. During a successful meeting, however, staff members used Post-it Notes to write their opinions about the attributes of Rentex's services that create value for customers' businesses. This resulted in the construction of the diagram on the next page.

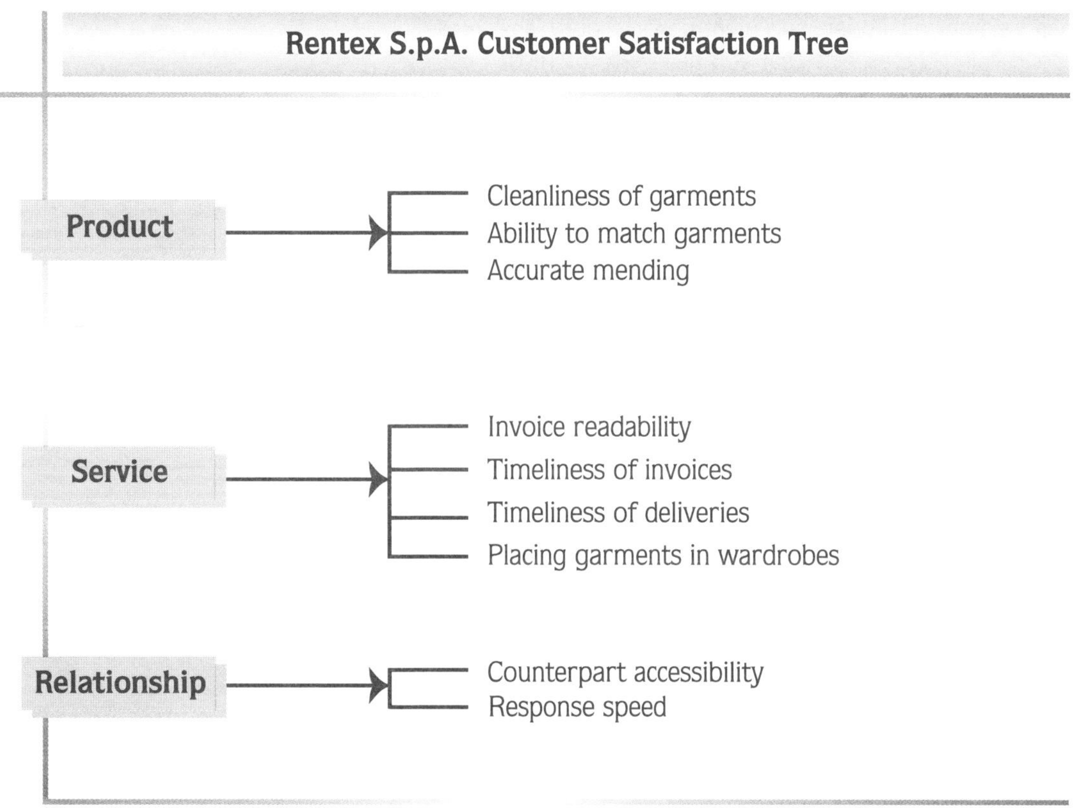

The elements for creating this diagram were provided by the business manager; members of Rentex's sales, manufacturing servicing, health servicing, and administration divisions; operators; and the quality assurance manager.

Rentex S.p.A.'s Customer Satisfaction Survey

The purpose of this questionnaire is to measure the level of product/service quality provided by Rentex S.p.A. Corporation. Your answers will help us implement, via our quality-enhancement process, our plans for improvements concerning the aspects that you believe to be most important for your success.

Instructions for completion:
Please provide your opinion on the importance of, and the degree of satisfaction you place on, the listed attributes by using a scale of 0 to 5, where 0 stands for "not important/low satisfaction" and 5 stands for "very important/high satisfaction."

Company name ______________________________

Address ______________________________

Phone______________________________

Fax______________________________

Date: ______________

E-mail address ______________________________

Person Interviewed:

Last name ______________________________

First name ______________________________

Type of product purchased ______________________________

	Importance	Satisfaction
1: PRODUCT		
1.1 Cleanliness of garments	5 4 3 2 1 0	5 4 3 2 1 0
1.2 Ability to match garments	5 4 3 2 1 0	5 4 3 2 1 0
1.3 Accurate mending	5 4 3 2 1 0	5 4 3 2 1 0
2: SERVICE		
2.1 Invoice readability	5 4 3 2 1 0	5 4 3 2 1 0
2.2 Timeliness of invoices	5 4 3 2 1 0	5 4 3 2 1 0
2.3 Timeliness of deliveries	5 4 3 2 1 0	5 4 3 2 1 0
2.3 Placement of garments in wardrobes	5 4 3 2 1 0	5 4 3 2 1 0
3: RATIO		
3.1 Counterpart accessibility	5 4 3 2 1 0	5 4 3 2 1 0
3.2 Response speed	5 4 3 2 1 0	5 4 3 2 1 0
4: OVERALL SATISFACTION WITH OUR CORPORATION		5 4 3 2 1 0

5: OTHER COMMENTS

5.1 Concerning the items mentioned above ______________________________

5.2 Pertaining to your specific preferences ______________________________

6: Will you purchase from our corporation in the future? ☐ yes ☐ no

7: Would you recommend our products/services to other business managers? ☐ yes ☐ no

Thank-you for your time and effort.
We will notify you of the results of our survey.

Customer Satisfaction

DATA COLLECTION:

Seventy-five corporate customers were directly interviewed for responses to the customer satisfaction survey. Data-collection activities were conducted from January 10 until March 14, 2000. These activities involved four staff members and the business manager.

COMPLAINT MANAGEMENT:

Rentex's complaint-management strengths lie in its continual customer contact. The company informs the customer, either by phone or by letter, of all decisions and provisions it takes to resolve complaints. The results of the actions taken are made known to everyone within the organization, an indication of its efficiency.

ACTIONS TAKEN:

The overall customer evaluations were positive. But the business manager decided to further invest in customer listening by creating a new position to handle customer service. Furthermore, Rentex has prepared a response card (see the sample on page 100) to give to every customer in the future.

Results of Customer Satisfaction Survey Conducted by Rentex S.p.A.

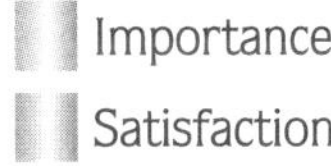

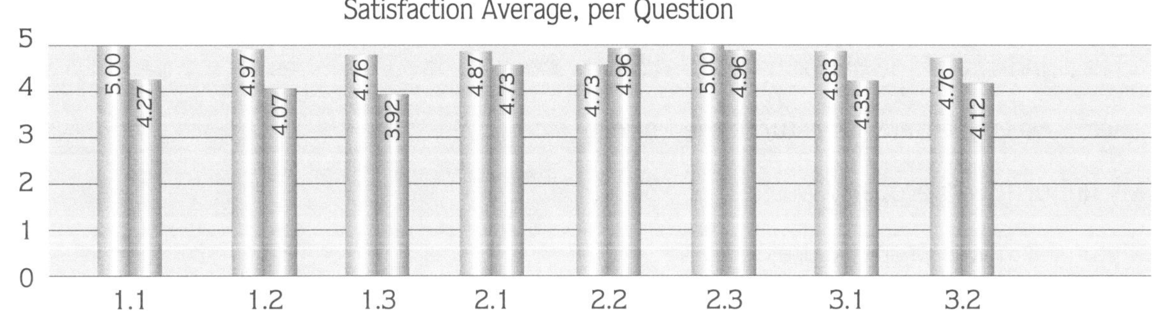

Questions
1.1 through 3.2

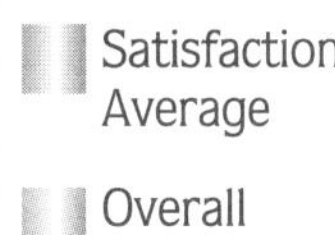

Comparision of Satisfaction Average and Overall Satisfaction

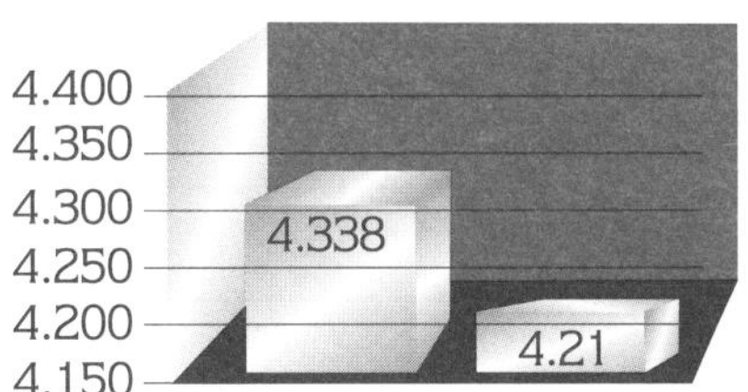

Question 6

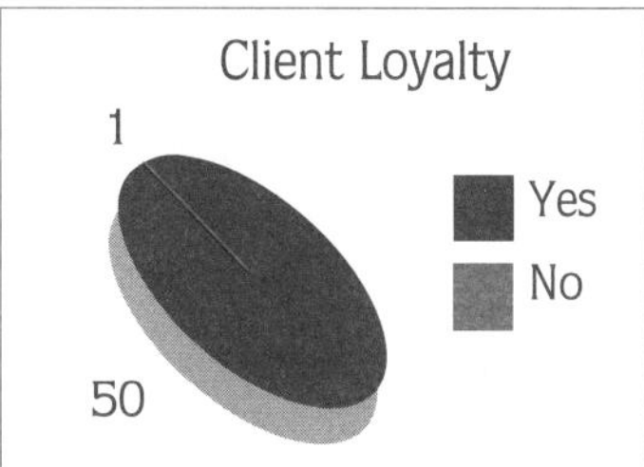

Rentex Industrial Laundry and Garment-Rental Wardrobe Service

We want to provide you with excellent service. Therefore, we are asking you to take just a few minutes of your time to help us better understand your perception of our services.

Date: ____________________

I could not find any of my uniforms on the conveyor belt. ☐ Yes ☐ No

☐ The conveyor belt always returns the uniform.

☐ My uniform was properly washed.

☐ My uniform was properly pressed.

☐ My torn uniform was properly mended.

____

____

Full name ____

Signature ____

Reply from the wardrobe service:____

____

____

Dal Cin S.p.A.

Business Description

Established in Milan in 1949, Dal Cin was one of the first companies in Europe to conduct research and production in all fields pertaining to the wine and beverage industries. The organization also conducts business in solid/liquid separation procedures for manufacturing industries (chemical, pharmaceutical, oil, and tanning) and in the preparation of products for agricultural use.

INDUSTRY: Wine products, industrial filters, and agricultural products

ANNUAL PROFIT: 2.7 million euros

NUMBER OF STAFF MEMBERS: 50

In October 1998, Dal Cin gained its Quality Certification in compliance with the UNI EN ISO 9001 Standard for the design, production, and sale of its entire range of products, both industrial and agricultural.

Dal Cin's ISO 9001 Standard Quality Certification for its wine products was the first certification ever given to a firm on Italian territory. (Source: www.dalcin.com)

Experimentation Method

PERSON INVOLVED: The business manager

EXPERIMENTATION STEPS:

SELF-EVALUATION ON LEADERSHIP: Dal Cin had a good average overall score of 8.8. The lowest score received was for point 1, for not conducting surveys to measure and monitor customer satisfaction. The highest scores received were for point 4 and points 6 through 9. Customer satisfaction is a key factor within the organization, and staff members are well acquainted with the different types of customers they serve and their behavior.

MEETING WITH STAFF: The business manager met with his staff members in a brief meeting, during which the principal attributes that customers normally appreciate in Dal Cin's products/services were discussed. The results of that meeting are summarized in the diagram on the next page.

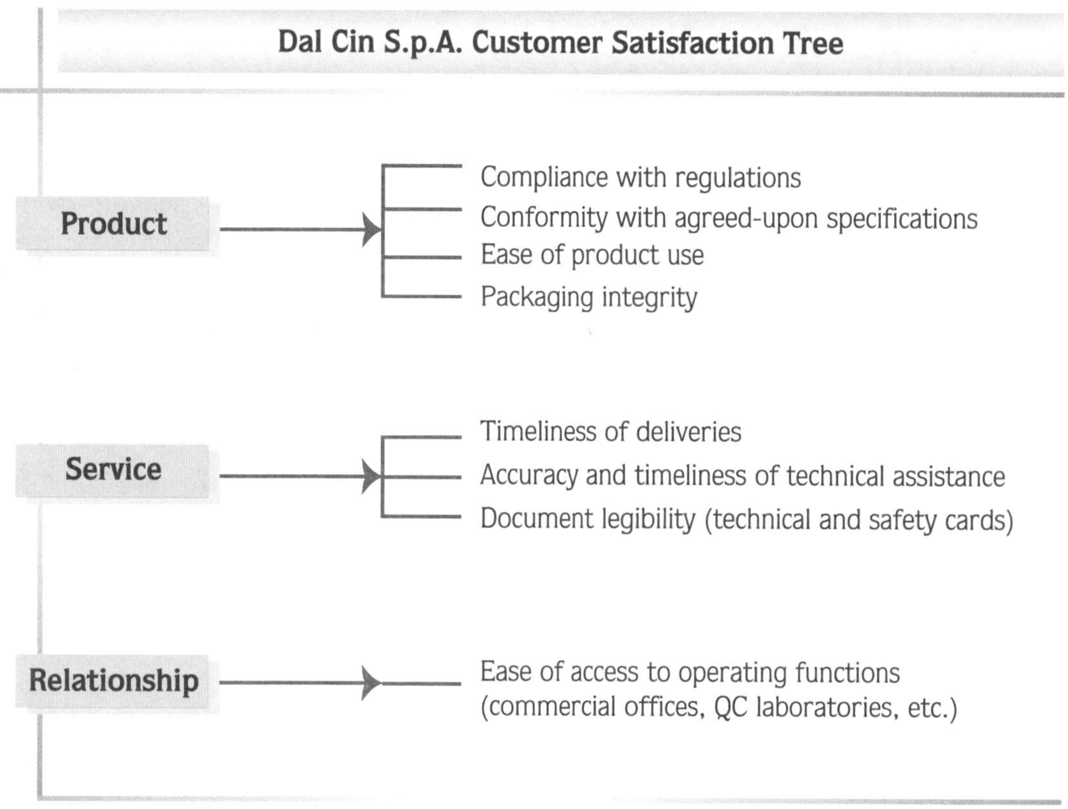

The elements for constructing this diagram were provided by Dal Cin's business manager and members of the following divisions: sales and commercial, administration, technical, logistics (quality assurance manager), and human resources (internal quality manager).

CUSTOMER SATISFACTION

THE COMMITMENT PLAN TO THE CUSTOMER:

The business manager planned various customer-satisfaction-related activities for the first half of 2000. Activities that were planned and carried out between January and March included customer segmentation, a general survey, data collection, and results processing. Beginning in April, customer response cards were included in product packages.

RESULTS OF THE GENERAL SURVEY:

The business manager gave the questionnaire to a group of customers; the global results (see page 106) were positive. They were divided according to product, service, and relationship. The lowest scores were given to item 1.3, ease of product use, and item 1.4, packaging integrity. Dal Cin promptly remedied its weaknesses by implementing corrective actions and quickly communicating them to its customers (see the letter on page 107).

Scheduled Surveys: 2000

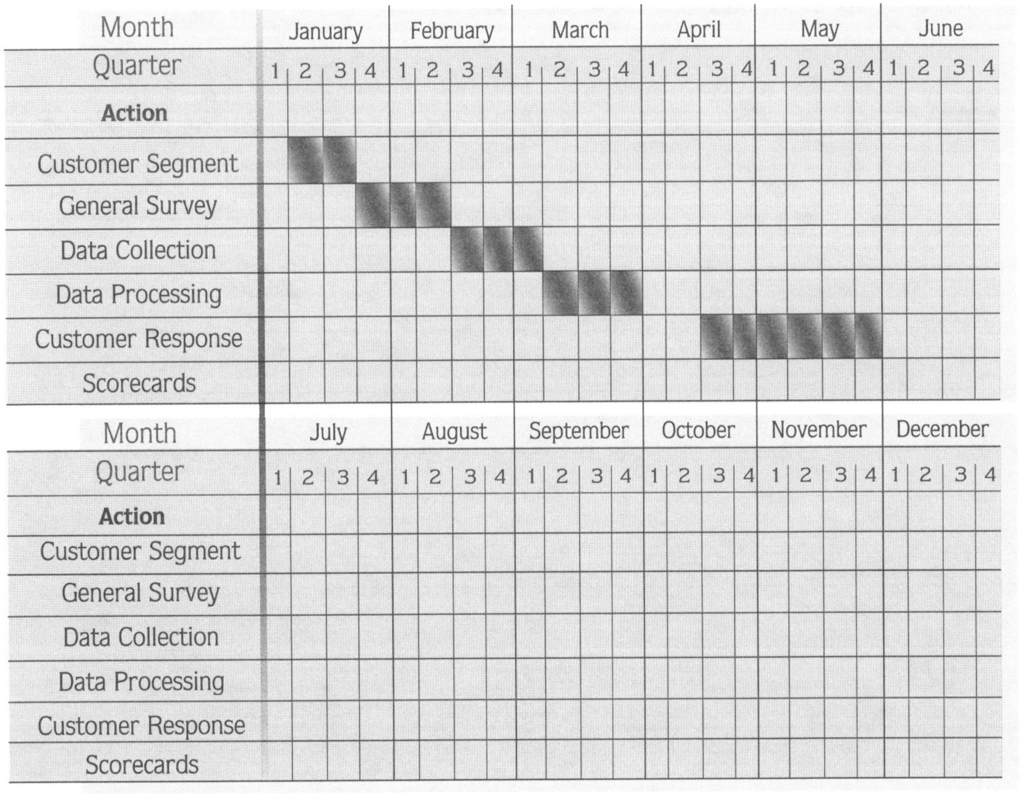

Month	January				February				March				April				May				June			
Quarter	1	2	3	4	1	2	3	4	1	2	3	4	1	2	3	4	1	2	3	4	1	2	3	4
Action																								
Customer Segment																								
General Survey																								
Data Collection																								
Data Processing																								
Customer Response																								
Scorecards																								

Month	July				August				September				October				November				December			
Quarter	1	2	3	4	1	2	3	4	1	2	3	4	1	2	3	4	1	2	3	4	1	2	3	4
Action																								
Customer Segment																								
General Survey																								
Data Collection																								
Data Processing																								
Customer Response																								
Scorecards																								

Dal Cin S.p.A.'s Customer Satisfaction Survey

The purpose of this questionnaire is to measure the level of product/service quality provided by Dal Cin Corporation. Your answers will help us implement, via our quality-improvement process, our plans for improvements concerning the aspects that you believe to be most important for your success.

Instructions for completion:
Please provide your opinion on the importance of, and the degree of satisfaction you place on, the listed attributes by using a scale of 0 to 5, where 0 stands for "not important/low satisfaction" and 5 stands for "very important/high satisfaction."

Company name ______________________________

Address ______________________________

Phone______________________________

Fax______________________________

E-mail address ______________________________

Person Interviewed:

Last name ______________________________

First name ______________________________

NOTE: All data we collect shall be used only for internal statistical purposes to implement our ISO 9001 Certified Quality System. Dissemination of data will be allowed only in an aggregate mode to prevent any possibility of identifying the individuals interviewed.

	Importance	Satisfaction
1: PRODUCT		
1.1 Compliance with regulations (reg. CE, HCCP, local legislation, etc.)	5 4 3 2 1 0	5 4 3 2 1 0
1.2 Compliance with agreed-upon specifications (if applicable)	5 4 3 2 1 0	5 4 3 2 1 0
1.3 Ease of product use	5 4 3 2 1 0	5 4 3 2 1 0
1.4 Packaging integrity (parcels, boxes, jars, paper bags, tanks, etc.)	5 4 3 2 1 0	5 4 3 2 1 0
2: SERVICE		
2.1 Invoice readability (DDT, invoices, technical and safety cards)	5 4 3 2 1 0	5 4 3 2 1 0
2.2 Timeliness of deliveries	5 4 3 2 1 0	5 4 3 2 1 0
2.3 Accuracy and timeliness of technical assistance (via both phone and field)	5 4 3 2 1 0	5 4 3 2 1 0
3: RELATIONSHIP		
3.1 Ease of access to operating functions (commercial offices, labs and technical offices, assistance)	5 4 3 2 1 0	5 4 3 2 1 0
4: OVERALL SATISFACTION WITH OUR CORPORATION		5 4 3 2 1 0

5: OTHER COMMENTS

5.1 Concerning the items mentioned above ______________________________

5.2 Pertaining to your specific preferences ______________________________

6: Will you purchase from our corporation in the future? ☐ yes ☐ no

7: Would you recommend our products/services to other business managers? ☐ yes ☐ no

Thank-you for your time and effort.
We will notify you of the results of our survey.

Results of Customer Satisfaction Survey Conducted by Dal Cin S.p.A.

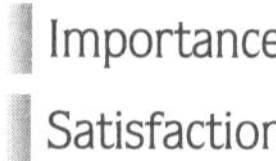

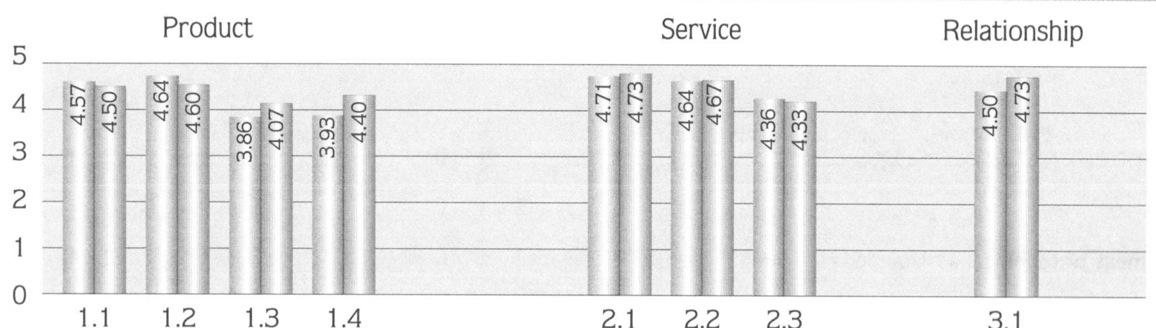

Overall Satisfaction for Questions 1.1 through 3.1

Question 6

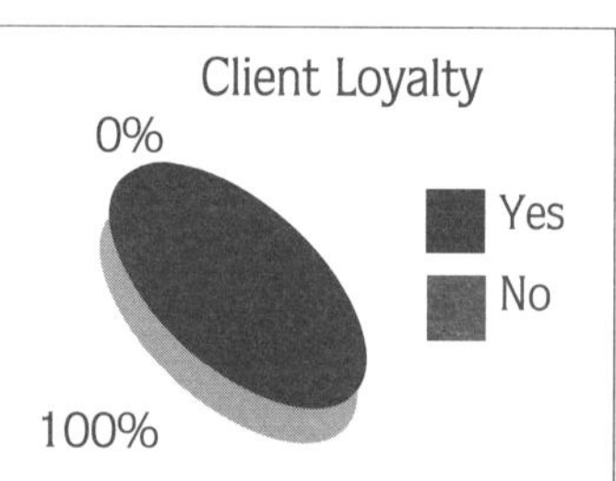

Question 7

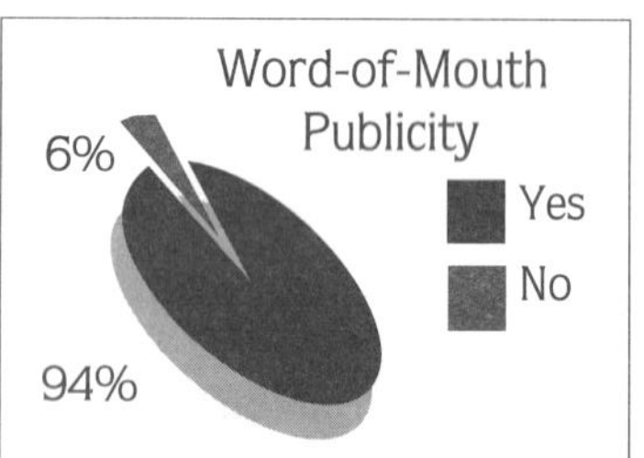

Sesto San Giovanni, April 20, 2000

Re: Customer Satisfaction Survey of February/March 2000

Dear Customer:

We thank you for the time you spent providing your answers to our survey. Careful analysis of the observations and suggestions received from the customers we contacted has led us to take action to improve our products and services.

Because of customer comments about our packaging typology, which we had been using for quite some time, we have completely revised the packaging. We hope that this change will serve you better.

You can review all the changes we have implemented based on suggestions we received from customers on our Web site, www.dalcin.com, in the "News" topic.

Best regards,

Dr. Daniele Moioli
Product Manager

Dal Cin Gildo S.p.A.

NOTES:

Suggested Reading

Busacca, B., M. Costabile, and E. Valdani. 1994. Customer Satisfaction. Milano: EGEA.

Cheaney, L., and M. Cotter. 1991. "Real People, Real Work." SPC Press, Inc.

Conca, M. G. 2000. "Quality Relationship: PMI and Vision 2000." Ricerca SDA Conversation Area Strategy from the Italian Consortium, Milan.

Conti, T. 1992. Constructing Total Quality. Sperling & Kupfer Editori, Milano.

Ghobadian, A., S. Speller, and M. Jones. 1994. "Service Quality: Concepts and Models." International Journal of Quality and Reliability Management, vol. 11, no. 9. American Management Association TARP (Technical Assistance Research Project).

Maslow, A. H. 1943. "A Theory of Human Motivation." Psychological Review, vol. 50.

Quaglino, G. P., ed. 1999. Leadership: New Profiles of Leaders of New Organizational Scenes. Raffaello Cortina Editore, Milano.

Tomiska, Y., ed. 1995. Customer Satisfaction Management. Il Sole 24, Ore, Milano.

Zeithaml, A., A. Parasuraman, and L. Berry. 1991. Quality Service. McGraw-Hill.

NOTES:

NOTES:

NOTES:

NOTES:

NOTES:

NOTES:

NOTES:

NOTES:

NOTES:

NOTES:

NOTES: